CHURCH SHIPS

A Handbook of Votive and Commemorative Models

by
BASIL HARLEY

The Canterbury Press
Norwich

© Basil Harley, MBE, FRSA, 1994
First published 1994 by The Canterbury Press Norwich
(a publishing imprint of Hymns Ancient & Modern Limited,
a registered charity)
St Mary's Works, St Mary's Plain,
Norwich, Norfolk, NR3 3BH

Basil Harley has asserted his right under the
Copyright, Designs and Patents Act, 1988, to be identified
as Author of this Work

British Library Cataloguing in Publication Data

A catalogue record for this book is available
from the British Library

ISBN 1-85311-094-9

*Typeset by Datix International Limited
Bungay, Suffolk and
Printed and bound in Great Britain by
St Edmondsbury Press Limited
Bury St Edmunds, Suffolk*

Contents

In Holy Trinity, Salcombe, Devon, the Brixham smack Heather Ann *hangs by a single wire to give life and movement to a well-loved model.*

Preface

The chance discovery of a glorious model of Sir Francis Drake's flagship *Bonaventure* in the Church of St Mary the Virgin in Painswick in Gloucestershire first fired my imagination to seek other church ships. My wife and I were paying a special visit to St Mary's to admire the impressive collection of embroidered kneelers when I was rivetted to see the *Bonaventure* displayed on the west wall of the north aisle. Although I knew that many churches in Scandinavia and Brittany were homes to a variety of votive and commemorative ship models I had not appreciated that they were also to be found in this country. As a result, I was stimulated to do some research into the survival of other church models, and although I make no claims that this is a fully comprehensive survey, I have brought together much hitherto scattered information and succeeded in revealing a number of previously neglected ship models.

All through childhood I was fascinated with model and miniature ships and boats. In later life my interest has developed and over the years I have designed and built a number of working model steam launches. The plans and construction details for these have been published in the model press, both here and in America, and many hundreds have been built by model makers all over the world. I also collect early toy and model boats many of which have the appeal and charm to be found in the naive and simple models made by sailors themselves on long and dangerous voyages.

The skills of the shipbuilders from medieval times until the present day have been supported by precise models, as well as drawings, to determine the complex shapes of the hull components. In the eighteenth and nineteenth centuries the Admiralty modelmakers were essential to our shipbuilding trade. The typical half model, mounted on a board, was marked to indicate the sizes and shapes to which timber, and later, metal sheets should be cut.

In the middle of the eighteenth century the Society for the Encouragement of Arts, Manufactures and Commerce pioneered a series of trials in which special model hulls were towed on long stretches of open water in an attempt to improve the design of warships. The experiments were not entirely satisfactory at the time but they marked the beginning of modern methods of model testing now in use all over the world.

The standards of modelmaking in church ships vary enormously. The best of them are first class examples of the modellers' skills in woodworking, metalcraft, painting and finishing. Many, however, are primarily decorative and sometimes have exaggerated features, such as thick spars, heavy rigging and oversized guns, so as to become virtual caricatures of their prototypes. These features helped to make the models stand out when seen from a distance in a large building or, occasionally, when they were carried in procession. I have no record of any of these church models ever being sailed on the water. Even those which are designed as practical, sailing, models are invariably preserved away from their true element.

The early vessels, modelled from measurements, drawings or direct observation have real historic value as witnesses of their time. The majority, often those with the greatest appeal to us today, are examples of true folk craft, made by devoted amateurs as expressions of their affection and deep feelings for the vessels they have re-created in miniature.

When visitors to a church first discover a model boat – and many of them are tucked away inconspicuously – the first questions asked are how old is it and why is it there? Frequently only the sketchiest details are given and often they are not even mentioned in the guide books. Perhaps the model commemorates a named ship or was given by a local sea captain for no stated reason. The relevance of some of the earlier ship models is sometimes in doubt but in most cases there is a story to be told. My researches have also revealed that the custom of donating ship models still continues and that many of the most attractive and interesting ones have been made and dedicated in the last thirty years. It is my object in this book to tell something of the background histories of these models, both the better-known and the obscure ones.

Sometimes the models have been made and donated for a very specific reason. That in Painswick Church was simply as an expression and reminder of the symbolic significance of the ship to the Christian faith. Others are purely votive models, given to fulfil a vow of thanksgiving, whereas many more are there to commemorate a ship, an event or a personality. Usually, however, the reasons stem from a mixture of all three.

In recognition of this I have organised the book somewhat arbitrarily into a number of sections. The treasures of those churches and chapels which are primarily of a symbolic and a votive nature are described in chapters two and three. The majority, those mainly of a commemorative nature, I have divided into sections reflecting the nature of the vessels themselves. Thus there are separate chapters devoted to mission ships and lifeboats, traders and fishing vessels and the more famous historic ships.

A few of the ship models have been found languishing unloved and in poor condition. Even so, there may still be more lurking in vestries, crypts and towers waiting to be re-discovered and brought back into the light. I hope that this book may give a new insight into the meaning and significance of these charming vessels so that many more may be discovered and identified.

THE COMPASROSE

The Compasrose is found in the nave of Canterbury Cathedral and in Washington Cathedral and is becoming universally identified with the family of Anglican/Episcopal Churches.

The Folkestone church ship is carried in procession from St Peter's to the Harbour annually on the occasion of the 'Blessing of the Fisheries'.
(Photo – Courtesy of Father Michael Houghton.)

Acknowledgements

I have been unable to visit all the places noted in this book but enquiries of friends, and letters to *Country Life*, the *Church Times*, the *Methodist Recorder*, *The Sign* magazine and many other publications, have resulted in a widespread correspondence with people who have a great regard and affection for the models which are displayed in their churches.

I have been overwhelmed by their kindness and generosity in giving me information and photographs and allowing me to examine and photograph many of their treasures for myself. I am both proud and sorry that there are too many people to thank individually but the following have been particularly helpful and generous with their time and patience.

Mrs Rosalind Butler of Warsash for personal recollections and photographs; the Revd Guy S. Cole of Bristol for his early encouragement and the notes of his own researches; Mrs Shirley Cordeau of Southwold P.C.C.; Mrs Muriel Costelloe for her help with the Wouldhave lifeboat model in South Shields; the Revd Canon Peter Delaney for permission to photograph the All Hallows-by-the-Tower models; Mr L.A. Haslett of Bristol for references in The Mariner's Mirror; the late Revd Canon Harold Heal and Commander J.E. Poulden concerning the Painswick *Bonaventure* and Mr A.D. Hutchings of Bexleyheath for much valuable background information. Mr W.T.C. Walker introduced me to St Monance. Particular thanks are due to Mrs Jean W. Kent for putting me in touch with the Tristan da Cunha islanders, and to Col. F.A. Manning and the Revd Will Mowll, a master model shipbuilder, who helped in many ways. Mr Martin Gilfeather of Fairlie, the Revd Canon Nicholas Frayling of Liverpool, Mr Jonathan Green, Mr Donald Long, Mrs Catherine Parkes, Mr Phillip Thomas of Glasgow, Mr Reg Snell of Lowestoft and the Revd Michael Houghton were among those who provided photographs.

I am much indebted for information and assistance given by – Mr G.B.L. Barr, York Minster; Mrs Sheila Beber, Edinburgh Cathedral; Dr Nicholas Bennett, Lincoln Cathedral; the Revd Canon Peter Brett, Canterbury Cathedral; Mr G. Fordham, Chatham Dockyard; the Revd Canon Glyn Jones, The Missions to Seamen; Mr J. Edwards, Aberdeen Maritime Museum; Mr Mark Lawrence, Scottish Fisheries Museum Trust; Mr Hugh Meller, National Trust; Mr John Orange, St Botolph's Library and Church Records, Boston; Mr L.C.K. Reynolds, Diocese of Norwich; Dr Alan Scarth, Merseyside Maritime Museum; Mr Simon Stephens, National Maritime Museum; Mr E.A.C. Tucker, Southwark

Cathedral; the Revd Peter Warland, HMS *Drake* and Mrs Janet Williams of the United Society for the Propagation of the Gospel; also to Hillside Fine Art, publishers of The Compasrose bookmark.

Among my other correspondents the following have been sources of much help and guidance – Mr W.J.C. Allen, The Revd Paul Abram, The Revd Jim Bates, Mr & Mrs Clive Brown, Mr Robin Craig, Mr Robert Crerar, Mr John Crowther, Mr Peter Dane, Pastor Fabricus, The Revd P.E. Fluck; Mr H. Gibson, Capt. J.A. Good, The Revd Canon, B.A. Hardy, Mr Richard Hunter, Mr Dick Knee, Mr A.L.Marshall, Miss K. McIntosh, Mr Joe Moss, Mrs P.I.C. Payne, Mrs Francis D. Richardson, Mrs Winifred Roper, Mr Michael Scott, Miss Dinah Smith, Mr Nicholas Thomas, Mr Frank Walker, Mr and Mrs E.P. Wanstall and Mr H.I.S. Williams.

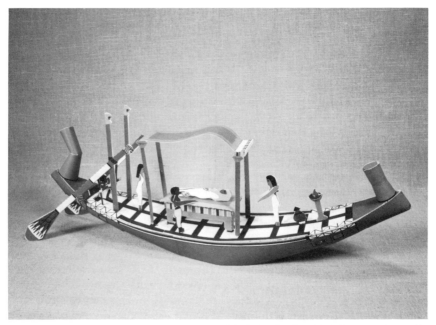

This paper cut-out toy funeral barge, published by the British Museum, shows the continuing popular interest in Egyptian boat symbolism.

I

Introduction

The Lord is my Pilot; I shall not drift.
He lighteth me across the dark waters;
He steereth me in deep channels;
He keepeth my log.
He guideth me by the Star of Holiness for His Name's sake.

Journeys by sea have always been hazardous and not to be undertaken lightly, and this has remained true even into our own century. The tragedy of the ill-fated *Titanic* in 1912 still has power to move us. Perhaps for this reason a voyage by ship has long been used as a symbolic representation of our spiritual journey through life as well as being one of the agents of rebirth. On the other hand, ships and boats have also been seen as the conquerors of the seas and, by extension, the means by which death and evil may be vanquished. Nowhere has this been more powerfully evident than to island peoples or other seafaring communities. Long before the advent of Christianity almost all early civilisations, particularly those bordering the Mediterranean Sea, had myths in which the ship played a central part.

In ancient Egypt the sun god Ra was represented as travelling across the heavens by day in a boat and through the underworld by night. There are many tomb models of funerary ships with the mummy and crew and mourners as well as more mundane boats to serve the deceased in the afterlife. A number of very fine models of ships of the eighteenth dynasty were discovered in the tomb of the boy king Tutankhamen.

Water was frequently seen as the route to the underworld and in Greek mythology Charon the ferryman carried the souls of the dead across the river Styx in his barge. As boats bear a superficial resemblance to both cradles and coffins numerous superstitious beliefs and practices have been associated with them, some of which persist to this day. There is much evidence of ship burial in prehistoric times in Scandinavia as well as here in Britain. Our best known example is at Sutton Hoo, and many examples of very early votive boats have also been discovered.

The National Museum of Wales has a late Bronze Age votive model of a boat that was found in a bog, which had formerly been a lake, at Caergwrle in Flintshire. It was discovered in 1820 and has since been the subject of much academic attention. Originally thought to have been of bog oak it is now known to be of shale. It is engraved with a formal design of waves, possibly stylized oars and eyes on the prow. All the incisions are filled with gold leaf. As the Museum observes, it is a very early example of late Bronze Age or early Iron Age communities making votive offerings in lakes or streams.

This primitive association of ships with religious observances and beliefs had a marked influence on early Christian boat symbolism. The book of Genesis describes God's commands to Noah to make an 'ark' or ship to save selected members of the human and the animal kingdom from drowning in the Flood. Noah's Ark is remarkably well documented in the Bible account, from its principal measurements to the timber – gopher wood – which was to be used in its construction. Wooden representations of Noah's Ark are known to have been made at the beginning of the seventeenth century. They do not seem to have appeared in model form in churches perhaps because the whole church was regarded as the Ark with its saving function. Model Arks achieved their greatest popularity as children's toys, mostly originating in Germany, during the nineteenth century. In Victorian England they were called 'Sunday toys' and were specially reserved for the restrained amusement considered suitable for that day.

In the New Testament water and boats take on an enhanced significance. Many of the concepts were familiar in the pagan world and were easily adapted to make them acceptable to the Christian converts. In the Gospels boats and fishing are mentioned many times as they were one of the chief occupations of the time in Palestine. The first disciples were drawn from among the fishermen round the shores of the Sea of Galilee. Jesus preached from a boat and he walked on the waters and stilled the storm. In St John's Gospel (21.1ff) the miraculous draught of fishes was undoubtedly the inspiration for many symbolic pictures. 'Jesus showed himself again to the disciples at the Sea of Tiberias'. Simon Peter and some others 'Went forth and entered into a ship immediately and that night they caught nothing'. As the risen Christ stood on the shore, unrecognized by the disciples, he asked if they had found fish and, on being told 'No' he said 'Cast the net on the right side of the ship and ye shall find. They cast therefore and now were not able to draw it up for the multitude of fishes.'

Not only the ships but also many of their fittings and equipment were seen to have symbolic significance. The masts and yard arms of the square riggers were reminiscent of the Cross. The complex timber construction of a hull was sometimes imitated when a church roof was built, so that worshippers felt themselves to be in an upturned boat something like Peggoty's house in Charles Dickens' novel *David Copper-*

In Queen Victoria's reign a Noah's Ark was a popular nursery toy reserved for playing with on Sundays. This one was made in Germany about 1900. (Photo – Courtesy of Sothebys Ltd.)

field. A famous example of this is the church in Rouen, in France, where the roof is in the shape of an upturned Viking ship. Nearer home is the barrel ceiling of Mortehoe Church in Devon which is also seen as an upturned ship.

Church buildings were sometimes referred to as St Peter's Ships and the anchor became a Christian symbol with its promise of peace and tranquillity in a safe anchorage after a long and perilous voyage, literally over the sea, metaphorically through life. The compass card, housed in the ship's binnacle whereby it is guided, appears in many forms. A decorative version, the Compasrose, is found in the nave of Canterbury Cathedral and in Washington Cathedral. In the past few years it has been adopted as the symbol of the Anglican Communion.

There are many medieval representations of church ships taking the form of paintings and carvings in wood and stone, as well as in stained glass. These vary in complexity and detail from simple scratch drawings

3

on walls and pillars (e.g. Blakeney and Cley-next-the-Sea in Norfolk and St Margaret-at-Cliffe in Kent) to beautifully carved bench ends. The pre-Norman church of St Mary, Stow-in-Lindsey in Lincolnshire has the earliest known scratch drawing in England of an oared sailing Viking ship. It dates from the late tenth century and can be seen on the south side of the chancel arch. The twelfth century font in Winchester Cathedral also has a very early example of this primitive marine art, and there are delightful medieval ship carvings in St Andrew's Church, Cullompton, Devon. Models and miniatures have always had great appeal, thus a three-dimensional model of a boat with men fishing, or perhaps Noah in his Ark with his family, would have had considerable significance for worshippers and helped to reinforce these stories in the minds of the early converts. So it was that such vessels became symbols of the church carrying the faithful to salvation.

The Nef is an interesting variant on the same theme. The word is used for the nave of a church but it is also an elaborate container, often of gold and silver, in the form of a model ship. Its secular use was to hold the lord's salt or table napkins at medieval banquets when it was treated with exaggerated respect. Nefs were also used in church ritual to hold incense, and became the forerunners of many boat-shaped serving vessels. Perhaps the most famous secular one in Britain is the Burghley Nef in the Victoria and Albert Museum. Another superb example is the Nef Reliquary of St Ursula in Rheims Cathedral. Here is a ship with golden planking, an anchor and enamelled sails. A golden statuette of St Ursula herself adorns the mast head and she is accompanied by her 'crew' of ten silver virgins.

On the Continent the display of ex-voto ship models and paintings in churches has a long history. The popular view that such practices were restricted to a devout peasantry is quite wrong. They have an appeal to the sophisticated as well as the ordinary worshipper and are as well represented in the churches of the predominantly Protestant Scandinavian countries as they are in the Roman Catholic ones of France, Spain, Portugal and Italy.

In the past few years they have been the focus of much academic attention. A survey published in France in 1978 listed 126 major places of worship in Western Europe possessing ship models, ranging from Bergen in Norway to Catane in Sicily. None at that time was recorded as existing in Britain. The same survey reported that there had been 18 marine exhibitions in France of which 11 were devoted exclusively to ex-voto models loaned by churches and cathedrals, and there have been four more since.

The oldest recorded church ship would seem to be the mid-fourteenth century model in the Maritime Museum in Rotterdam. If genuine it anticipates by some two hundred years the Ashmolean Museum ship (see page 17). Although it was found in New York in the early 1930s, it was acquired by Mr D.G. van Beuningen of Rotterdam and loaned by him to the Prins Hendrik Museum where it has since been the subject of prolonged study. Prior to its appearance in the United States it had hung for centuries under the roof beams of a chapel in the Catalonian seaside town of Mataro. There were many ex-voto models in Spanish churches and chapels and it was not unusual for them to come into the hands of private people. It has been suggested that this one belonged to an important Spanish family who sold it to a dealer in New York. The model has a built hull, ie: it was not carved from a solid block, and although it had three masts when discovered, research has shown that originally there was only one and someone in the intervening centuries brought it up to date. It has now been restored.

Although the ex-voto model is typical of Continental custom nevertheless many churches in Britain possess a surprising variety of boat and ship models which have been donated for varying reasons. Here they are usually a focus for prayer and meditation whereas on the Continent they tend to be thank offerings to the Virgin or the saints for the relief of distress or for favours received. Usually they will be found suspended from the roof, often in the centre of the nave, or occasionally hidden away in a dark corner whilst others may be displayed on walls. Some may even be in glass cases. Sometimes they are quite ancient models, though there are many which have been made comparatively recently. The majority are three-dimensional miniature ships though there is at least one example of a real ship – or at least parts of one – in a church in Sussex. A few of the ship models are actually outside churches rather than inside them, usually masquerading as solid and imposing windvanes on towers and spires. In some cases the earlier ones are now cared for in museums, notably a fine authenticated 17th century votive model dating from 1689 preserved in the Maritime Museum in Aberdeen.

This is the background to the symbolic, to the commemorative and to the votive model boats and ships in British churches and cathedrals which are so often regarded with great affection by incumbents and worshippers alike. Usually the reasons for their display are self-evident, for instance, the recent votive ship in Bletchingley Church records the gratitude of the people of Tristan da Cunha when they were evacuated to Britain after the volcano erupted on their island. A model and the ship's bell commemorates HMS *Canterbury* in the south west transept of Canterbury Cathedral. In some cases, as in Painswick Church in Gloucestershire in the heart of the Cotswolds, the symbolic element takes precedence.

2

The Ship as a Christian Symbol

One of the most striking examples of the ship motif as a Christian symbol is the seaward front of St Leonard's Parish Church at St Leonards-on-Sea, Sussex. The original church, by James and Decimus Burton dating from 1834, was destroyed by a V-1 flying bomb in 1944. The new one, dedicated in 1956, has a boat-shaped western entrance beneath the tower and a marble fish on the chancel floor. The first rector, Canon C.C. Griffiths, suggested that the pulpit be in the form of a replica of the boat from which Jesus taught on the Sea of Galilee. And it is this, made in 1956 by a Jewish carpenter in a fishing village on the shores of the Sea of Galilee, which dominates the nave. Alongside it is a ship's binnacle which serves as the lectern – as the ship is guided by the compass so the Church takes its bearings from the Bible. This use of a binnacle is uncommon but there is another in the Seaman's Chapel in the Parish Church of St Mary, Southampton.

Ship models are most frequently displayed in churches in coastal towns and villages. However, one of the most impressive of those which are primarily symbolic is the fine model, far from the sea, of Sir Francis Drake's flagship *Bonaventure* on the west wall of the north aisle in the Parish Church of St Mary, Painswick, in the Cotswolds.

The *Bonaventure* was built in 1580 and was 'one of that noble company of the Queen's ships' which played their parts in many engagements between 1580 and 1600, including the defeat of the Armada in 1588. The model was presented to the church in 1971 by Commander J. Edward Poulden, a former churchwarden, as a symbol of the Church which sails unharmed through all perils. The model was built about 1885 in Bristol by James Farrier, an amateur ship modeller, to a scale of 1/25 (it is over six feet long) and had been in Commander Poulden's family for many years. He acquired it from his grandparents when a boy and latterly spent some three years restoring it before the vicar asked him if he would present it to the church.

It was from the *Bonaventure* that Sir Francis Drake wrote the letter containing the sentence from which his so-called prayer was derived. 'There must be a begynnyng of any great matter, but the contenewing unto the end untyll it be thoroughly ffynyshed yeldes the trew glory.'

Ship symbolism on the west front of the Parish Church of St Leonards-on-Sea.

The boat-shaped pulpit in St Leonard's was made in 1956 by a Jewish carpenter working in a village on the Sea of Galilee.

A ship's binnacle forms the lectern in St Leonard's. As the ship is steered by the compass, so the Church is guided by the Bible.

This splendid model of Sir Francis Drake's flagship Bonaventure *measures over six feet long. It is in St Mary's Church, Painswick, Gloucestershire.*

In 1935 a massive model of the *Mauretania*, over twelve feet long, was presented to Winchester Cathedral by Sir Thomas Royden of the Cunard-White Star Company. The Southampton Master Mariners' Club had initiated an annual shipping festival service and the model was given to act as a focal point. One of the most famous of the great Transatlantic liners of the 1920s and 1930s the *Mauretania* model was the first instance of a modern liner being used as a church ship. It was dedicated by Dr Cyril Garbett, the then Bishop of Winchester. Whilst it had its value as a symbol it is perhaps not surprising that so large a model might come to be regarded as an embarrassment and in 1966 the cathedral authorities sold it to the National Maritime Museum at Greenwich where it is still on display. Although there is no maker's nameplate it is thought to be a builder's model, made to the scale of a quarter of an inch to the foot.

A similar presentation by a shipping magnate was the SS *Vale of Pickering* given in 1936 to York Minster by Sir Christopher Furness. This is a model of the 2,550 tons cargo vessel built in 1922 by the Furness Shipbuilding Co of Haverton Hill and owned by the Vale Shipping Co of Middlesborough. It used to be in the Nave but in recent years it was kept

9

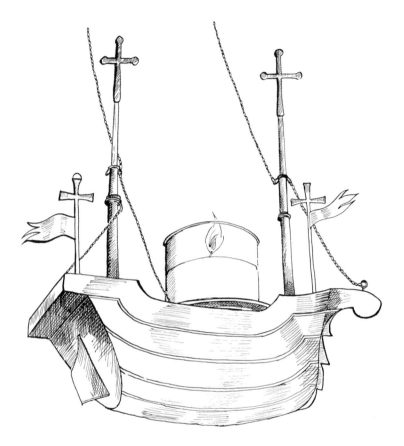

The sanctuary lamp in the Holy House in the shrine of Our Lady of Walsingham. The silver model is engraved on the stern 'Star of the Sea'.

in the Chapter House vestibule. *The Vale of Pickering* is a large model, some 6 feet 6 inches long bearing the date 1922, and is probably a builders' model. A few years ago it was transferred to St William's College, a large and important medieval building used by various Minster departments and standing near the east end of the Minster. It is currently in the Maclagan Hall in the College, a room which is normally open to the public.

The High Anglican church of Our Lady of Walsingham in Norfolk has a number of ship models. In the Holy House, a small shrine built within the Shrine Church, is a sanctuary lamp in the form of an early carrack. The hull forms the container for oil but it is now lit electrically. It is very simply, almost crudely, made in a silvery metal and is engraved on the stern 'Star of the Sea'. It hangs in front of the statue of Our Lady with other more conventional lamps and was probably made in the 1930s especially for the shrine. The outside walls of the Holy House, still of course, within the Church, have a number of rough blocks of stone set in them with carved names, *St Pauls, Branham, Christ Church* etc, looking as though they have been taken from earlier buildings. One, projecting far enough to form a bracket, having *Hickling P* carved upon it, is the support for an early model of a nineteenth century three masted schooner. It is probably an armed merchantman, but sadly, when seen some time ago, had a badly damaged bowsprit. Elsewhere there are other symbolic models on the walls, including a rather later miniature of a Transatlantic liner.

Ship weathervanes are among the most popular Christian symbols though more secular buildings than churches are adorned with them. The church of St Mary in Nefyn, Gwynedd, has had a large schooner weathervane, measuring over six feet long, for over half a century. The church was de-consecrated about twelve years ago and today is used as the local maritime museum. Many brigs and brigantines were built on the beach at Nefyn and the church/museum has a collection of models of them. It is only open in the summer months.

Most ship weathervanes are simple silhouette metal cut-outs and they represent a huge range of vessels from the fifteenth to the nineteenth centuries, among them warships, merchantmen, racing yachts and fishing boats. Since these are not strictly models two examples only are quoted to exemplify the type. There is a delightful vane in the form of a three-masted top-sail schooner on the cupola surmounting the Holy Cross Chapel which is now the town museum in the little port of Watchet in Somerset. This bears the date 1987 and represents one of the best modern designs. Another is the sailing ship on the south-east turret of Ilfracombe's parish church. It was made much earlier, presumably about 1900, when it was first installed after the church was rebuilt to the designs of the architect who was also responsible for the Methodist and United Reformed Emanuel Church in the same town.

Although from a distance it looks like a three-dimensional model the Ilfracombe ship is really flat. The three-dimensional weathervanes form a separate category and are substantially built models, usually of copper and frequently gilded, designed to ride out the worst storms on their pinnacles, towers and steeples. Fairlie Parish Church in Ayrshire is probably unique in having a wooden model of a yacht for the windvane. She is the yawl *Latifa*, a Hebrew word meaning 'most beautiful'. The

A recent ship windvane in the Somerset village of Watchet.

This sailing ship has adorned the south-west turret of Ilfracombe Parish Church since about 1900.

original was designed in 1936 by William Fife as an ocean racer and she still sails the Carribean and the Mediterranean. The gilded wooden model with its brass rigging was recently taken down and repaired. The photograph shows her being replaced on the spire of Fairlie church in 1991.

The best known of the three-dimensional models is the famous 'Golden Barque', the windvane on the tower and cupola of Portsmouth Cathedral. Until 1927 this was the parish church of St Thomas of Canterbury when it was raised to cathedral status. The original model of the ship, eagerly looked for by generations of seamen returning home, graced the cupola from 1710 until 1954 when it was blown down in the December gales. It has been suggested that it was originally erected in 1710 to celebrate a financial triumph of the churchwardens over their vicar. Restoration was undertaken in 1958 by the members of the Cathedral's Business Men's committee and today it is displayed in the nave, mounted on a plinth of oak taken from the *Victory*. It is most impressive, being some five feet long. The huge ensign at the stern ensures that she turns into the wind, conventionally indicating the direction from which it is blowing. We all accept that the prow and the bowsprit of a ship on a weathervane points towards the wind whereas in practice the wind will always blow from nearer the stern to drive it forwards.

The disaster of 1954 was not the first time it had been down. It is made of gilded copper and on the deck are two plaques, about five inches square, which record earlier repairs. That on the foredeck says, 'Repaired and regilded by E. Grey; W. Grant, Vicar 1873' The aft deck plaque reads 'Repaired by G. Russell, Coppersmith, re-gilded by E.T. Foster under the superintendance of Harold Wyllie in June 1912. R.S. Medlicott, Vicar.' Today, a modern replica maintains the tradition of a 'Golden Barque' on the cathedral cupola.

A re-gilded wooden model of the yawl Latifa *being erected on the spire of Fairlie church in Ayrshire in 1991.* (*Photo – Courtesy of Martin Gilfeather.*)

The famous 'Golden Barque', an eighteenth century windvane which is now in the nave of Portsmouth Cathedral. A modern replica has replaced it on the tower.

Until fairly recently there was a survival of a pre-Christian superstition connected with this model. Whenever it was brought down for renovation mothers of the parish invoked an ancient ritual by placing their youngsters in the hull for a few minutes to ensure that in later life they would not be drowned at sea. At some time in the past there were as many as six model ships hanging in the cathedral. They were still there until after the last war but seem to have disappeared when the extensions and reconstruction began. It is not known what happened to them.

Mr W.L. Wyllie, a member of the family who organised the 1912 repair of the windvane also made the model of a *Mary Rose* (not *the* Mary Rose) which hangs above the memorial to Admiral Kempthorne. It is about four feet long and was made from wood given by a Portsmouth-born New Zealander, Mr Clement Langford. It was carried in procession to the church for its presentation in 1929, the 250th anniversary of the Admiral's death. It is really more of a commemorative model adding interest to the

memorial plaque which reads – 'Here lyeth interred the body of Sir John Kempthorne, Knight, who had ye honour to wear several flags in several commands in his Majesty's service, and hath fought several battles at sea for his King and Country and dyed Commissioner of His Majesty's Navy at Portsmouth the 19th day of October 1679 being aged 59 yeares.' The *Mary Rose* was his last command.

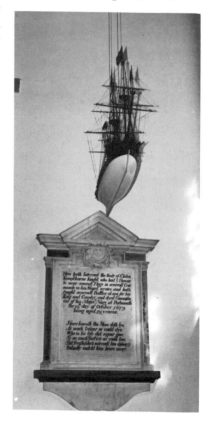

Admiral Sir John Kempthorne's seventeenth century monument in Portsmouth Cathedral with a later model of his last command, a Mary Rose, *hung to commemorate the 300th anniversary of his death.*

3

Votive Ships

Votive objects are those which are offered and dedicated in fulfilment of vows. They are usually small and may be replicas of almost anything. Any pre-historic artifact considered by archaeologists to have religious connotations – or those for which they can ascribe no useful purpose – are usually labelled votive objects. This is true of the Late Bronze Age model of a boat in the National Museum of Wales, and with even greater justification, the Egyptian model of a funeral boat, made of painted wood and dating from about 1900 BC, in the British Museum. Miniatures of everyday objects have always been of great interest and through the ages such things as houses, furniture, carriages and soldiers have been made, often of costly materials such as gold and silver, as 'princely playthings' or as ornaments. Boat and ship models have also been made for these purposes as well as being aids to shipbuilders. A monument in Burseldon Church in Hampshire to Philemon Ewer, an eighteenth century shipbuilder,

The Monument to Philomon Ewer, an eighteenth century shipbuilder on the Hamble river in Hampshire, incorporates this half-model of one of his ships.

This small armed merchantman dating from about 1605–1630 is one of the earliest surviving altar ships. It is in the Tradescant Room at the Ashmolean Museum in Oxford. (Photo – Courtesy of the Ashmolean Museum, Oxford.)

depicts a stone half-model which was used in the construction of one of his ships.

We cannot be sure when votive models first appeared in British churches. There appears to be none still in situ that were made before the middle of the eighteenth century and the very few earlier ones are now cared for in museums, in view of their interest for marine historians as well as to ensure their preservation in controlled conditions. It is rare for a church ship in a museum to have a proven provenance and attributions frequently have to be made on the evidence of date and quality of workmanship. An early model judged to have been sailor made and of a somewhat heavy construction is often considered to have been a church ship even in the absence of any documentary support. A good exmple of this is the mid-seventeenth century model in the Tradescant Collection in the Ashmolean Museum in Oxford which has been the subject of much speculation and expert examination.

The model is the surviving one of two recorded in the Tradescant's catalogue in 1685 and is considered to be the earliest extant in Britain.

The original Latin, translated, reads, 'Two wrecked ships, precisely modelled, equipped with various pieces of artillery, elaborately made out of wood'. The hull measures 2 feet long, is carved from solid oak and has a round bow with a long decorated beak-head surmounted by a decorative scroll. The artillery with which it is equipped consists of six broadside guns with two bow chasers and two stern chasers. The consensus is that it is a broadly conceived model, rather better than sailor made, of a small armed merchant ship C. 1605–1630. It is on display in the Tradescant Room of the Museum and is referred to on the descriptive label as an altar ship.

A mid-eighteenth century model in the Merseyside Maritime Museum is also classed as a church ship. This is more delicately built and is catalogued as a 'Votive Ship, One Hundred Gun, Three-decker Warship'. This substantial model measures 5 feet $7\frac{1}{2}$ inches overall and probably dates from between 1720 and 1760. Originally suspended, possibly over an altar, by a single rope attached to the hull amidships it has been fitted latterly with two metal slings. The hull is of yellow birch and most of the fittings are made from pine. It is sailor made, being true to type rather than true to scale. There is a crowned lion figurehead bearing traces of gilding and the rest of the vessel was brightly coloured to make an impact when viewed from a distance. For the same reason the size of the guns has been exaggerated. There is a group of figures on deck to represent the crew. The museum acquired it in 1932 at an auction of the contents of Sir Arthur du Cros' home, Craigwell House in Sussex, but it seems to have been originally owned by the Earl of Wemyss. He apparently bought it in 1916 but there is no record of it before then.

Almost all such ships were given in acknowledgement of deliverance from shipwreck or other perils at sea. In the narrow sense the offering of a ship model or anything else in fulfillment of a vow implied bargaining with God – a concept much discouraged by Protestantism. However, a votive object is usually interpreted as a thank-offering for prayers answered. This applies to most church ships though in many cases the symbolic or commemorative aspects take precedence. Those considered strictly as votive have been offerings made by individuals or groups who had overwhelming reasons for gratitude to God.

The Museum in Whitby, on the Yorkshire coast, established in 1823 by the Whitby Literary and Philosophical Society which still runs it, has just such a votive model now in store. It is thought to be Portugese and at present is in too poor condition to be exhibited. Nevertheless, it is to be restored and when that is being done hopefully more will be learned about its provenance and purpose. For example, any marks or eyes on the deck to which ropes or chains could have been fixed to enable a vessel to be hung from a roof is usually considered conclusive evidence that it has been a church ship at some period in its life.

Another foreign model is the well-known Dutch warship in the National Maritime Museum, Greenwich. This is a contemporary votive model of a two-decker ship of 28–32 guns dating from the mid-seventeenth century. It is a robustly built version of a vessel of some 240 tons burden which measured about 107 feet long. The museum considers that, although the date of 1657 appears on the stem of the model, the very long head and some features of the rigging suggest that it was built some years earlier.

The Museum of Transport in Glasgow also has a Dutch model described as a votive ship. She is the *Leefop Hoop*, built about 1770. The model is made of wood to 1/48 scale and measures about 2 feet 9 inches long. It is somewhat heavily constructed and hence is considered to be a contemporary sailor's model. Another in the collection is also thought to have been made as a votive offering. This is a model of the *Prince William*, formerly known as the *Guipuiscorna*, a 3rd-rate warship taken as a prize from the Spanish in 1781. It was at one time the property of Admiral Sir T. Livingston.

There is a votive ship in the outstanding collection of models gathered by Miss Rosalie Caroline Chichester in Arlington Court, Devonshire, which is now in the care of the National Trust. Miss Chichester was born in 1865, the only daughter of Sir Bruce and Lady Chichester. From early childhood she developed a love for the sea and all things nautical. After her parents' death she lived alone in Arlington Court for forty years until her own death in 1949. During this time she collected over thirty five fine bone model ships made in the early years of the nineteenth century by French prisoners of war, in addition to large numbers of other models, many of them specially commissioned.

Among the largest in the Chichester Collection is the impressive HMS *Princess Louisa* measuring something over five feet long overall. She is a 4th rate English man-of-war mounting 48 guns and dating from about 1750. In view of her rather heavy construction and over-scale detailing she is described by the National Trust as a church ship. She takes pride of place in the Lobby which is filled with ship models including a beautiful model of *Gypsy Moth IV* in which Miss Chichester's step-nephew, Sir Francis Chichester, made his epic voyage round the world in 1966-67. The original *Princess Louisa* was lost in 1736 and it is possible that the model was made as a votive memorial to her.

Whilst there are few serious reasons to question the attributions of any of these museum ships there is no doubt at all about the credentials of Aberdeen Maritime Museum's famous and much revered 17th century votive model. Affectionately known for centuries as 'The Schip' this also is of Dutch origin. There is documentary evidence that it was made in Holland and presented to the Shipmaster's Society, or The Seamen's Box of Aberdeen, in 1689. In 1670 the Society had received permission from the local magistracy to erect, at its own expense, a loft or gallery in the 'Quire at the west end of St Nicholas Church'. This was where the various seafaring members of the Society assembled for worship. There is a memorandum recording that in 1689 Captain Alexander Mackie 'had gifted ane ship to the Loft and did Hinge the same at his charge'. This was 'The Schip' and it was hung in front of the Seamen's loft until the church was restored in 1836. Thereafter there is reason to believe that the model was moved to the Society's new premises, 22 Regent Quay, which they acquired in 1840. It was when this building was sold in 1971 that the treasures, including 'The Schip', came into the care of the Aberdeen Maritime Museum. It has now been restored to its original form as a fifth rate Dutch warship.

HMS Princess Louisa *is a model of a 4th-rate English man-of-war dating from about 1750. She is recorded as a 'church ship' and is one of the outstanding models in the Chichester Collection at Arlington Court, Devonshire, now in the care of the National Trust.*

This is 'The Schip', a Dutch model which was first hung in St Nicholas' Church,
Aberdeen in 1689. It is now in the Maritime Museum and this picture is reproduced
by courtesy of the City of Aberdeen, Art Gallery and Museums Collection.

There was another votive model, the *Bon Accord*, which had also
belonged to the Society and had hung in St Paul's Episcopal Chapel since
1739 until it, too, was removed to Regent Quay. She was also a fully
rigged man-of-war but has subsequently been lost. In passing, it is
interesting that many of the early votive vessels were either armed
merchantmen or warships. There was felt to be no incongruity in having
fully armed vessels offered in fulfillment of vows in God's house.

Three other church ships are still extant in Aberdeen, two of them in
their original churches and one which hopefully will again return to its
previous place when both ship and church have been restored. They are

early nineteenth century models and all three apparently owe their exist-ence to one man. James Welsh was a man of many skills, among others he was a stone mason, an artist and a woodcarver. He was a devout Christian and a member of St Clement's Parish Church which had been built in 1828 on the site of an earlier one. A votive ship in the church was first recorded in 1889 when it was taken away for repair. It was attributed to James Welsh and it remained in the church until it was disbanded in 1987. During the latter days of the church it had been the incumbent's habit to loan the 'Old Ship', as it was called, to the College of Commerce for use in drawing lessons. As a result it was lost for a number of years until located recently by Lys Wyness and identified as a model of the warship HMS *Belvedera*. Built at Deptford in 1809 she was a regular visitor to Aberdeen harbour. Being in need of care, the model was taken to the Maritime Museum for restoration. The church is similarly undergo-ing considerable restoration and there is every intention that the two will be re-united.

There is another of Welsh's models in Nigg Parish Church. This is the *Phesdo*, presumably made and given to mark the completion of the church in 1829. It is a model of a three-masted, fully-rigged frigate and was presented to the church by a Captain Affleck. Inside is a paper which reads 'James Welsh, Shipbuilder, Aberdeen'. Since Welsh was not a full-sized shipbuilder this must refer to the model. It is still hanging in its original place in the church, looking in remarkably good condition for its age.

In the early nineteenth century a Dr James Kidd was a very popular and much revered preacher. He was the vicar of Denburn Parish Church and attracted large congregations to his somewhat austere church. Among his large family was his daughter Agnes who, in 1814, married a sea captain, James Oswald. It is not known whether one of his vessels bore her name but James Welsh, who admired Dr Kidd, made the model *Agnes Oswald* and dedicated it to her in 1830. Here again is a model of an armed merchantman which was hung in the church where it is still treasured today.

The fourteenth century Parish Church of St Monance, in Fife, is one of the most beautifully situated of all our sea side churches, dramatically poised high on the cliffs. Pride of place among its furnishings is a fine votive model of a square-rigged Royal Navy frigate of about 130 tons burthen, some 4 feet long. This hangs high up under the south transept archway and dates from about 1800. A local man, Captain Marr, was the captain of the (un-named) frigate when he was successful in winning prize money in some of its engagements. Out of gratitude some of the money was spent on commissioning the model which Captain Marr presented to the church 'to honour his seamen and to the Glory of God'. Recently another model has been given and hangs under the north transept archway. It is a model of a locally built fishing boat and was made in 1908, though nothing more is known about it.

Still in Fife, another massively built model of what seems to be a Dutch man–of–war dating from the early eighteenth century is in the Parish Church of All Saints in St Andrews. It is un-named, fully rigged with sails set and 32 guns uncovered. Hanging in the traditional way in the north-west corner of the nave it was presented in 1954 in memory of the novelist Sir Hugh Walpole by his sister Dr Dorothea Walpole. The model had belonged to Sir Hugh and for many years was kept in his study. The Fitz Park Museum in Keswick has a watercolour painting described in Rupert Hart-Davies' book 'Hugh Walpole' as a 'watercolour sketch of the top library at Brackenburn by D.B. Martin'. This shows the model sitting in one of the windows. It would appear that this was originally a votive model, removed from its original church for reasons unknown, which was somehow acquired by Sir Hugh and subsequently given to St Andrew's as a memorial ship.

The Parish Church of St Cuthbert in Saltcoats, Ardrossan, is the custodian of another sailor made model which dates from the early nineteenth century. A Mr William Dunlop made it in 1804 and gave it to the then parish church. Originally the model hung from a ceiling beneath the points of the compass done in relief work. The church was closed in 1908 and replaced by the present building to which the model was moved. William Dunlop's home town was Saltcoats and he was a gunner's mate on HMS *St Joseph*. It is said that he had a narrow escape from death when a shot passed over him while he was in his hammock. His model, made when he was at sea, is of a first-rate warship but, as with many sailor made models, there is some doubt about which vessel it is intended to represent. Today it is called the *Caledonia* which was a 50-gun frigate but earlier histories say it was modelled on the *San Joseef* which was captured by Lord Nelson from the Spanish in 1797 and this seems to be the more likely attribution. True scale accuracy was not rated highly by the sailors who made these models. They wanted to capture the 'feel' of their ships and in this they were often very successful.

A model that has sparked off some controversy in recent years is the Frigate hanging in the West Church, Greenock. A Sailors' Gallery was established in the church as early as 1698 and a model frigate was hung in it. This was reputed to have been made from a piece of wood from a wreck from the Spanish Armada. It remained in the gallery until it fell to pieces on being removed in 1856. For the next hundred years other models replaced it and in 1957 there was a lively correspondence in the local press as to whether the present one was the third or the fourth in line. It was at this time that it was overhauled, cleaned and re-painted by Commander James Munro, a member of the congregation. As well as putting newspaper cuttings on board relating to its history, Commander Munro also added a note about the restoration work that had been done, placed in an aluminium tube lashed to the deck. His father had done some work on the model in 1926 and it was he who got Dan McNeil, a modelmaker employed by Caird's Yard, to replace some of the rigging. The note continues 'Commander Munro has followed this precedent, so now the little frigate has three periods of rigging which an expert can trace. For a short time the frigate was placed on the cutty-stool in front of the Communion Table and was the theme of an address by Mr Morrison to the Youth Organisations'. This is a particularly interesting example of the continuing regard that congregations have for their ship models, in this case spanning three centuries, even if the Greenock frigate reminds us of the classic case of the 'original' Grandfather's axe which had had three new handles and two new heads.

Until 1993 there was a model of a very early vessel in the old port of Fordwich in Kent. The little town lies about three miles below Canterbury on the River Stour. In medieval times it was one of the Cinque Ports – or, to be precise, a Member of the Cinque Port of Sandwich – but it has long been isolated from the sea owing to geographical changes. The town is still conscious of its historical importance as a port and, as Lieut-Commander Arthur H. Waite RNR writes in the book *Fordwich – the lost port*, 'It is appropriate that Fordwich as the ancient port of Canterbury should have a model of a ship in its church.' Accordingly, in 1936 a model of a late 15th century carrack was made by Mr William Leighton, assisted by some local ex-Service men, to be hung in St Mary the Virgin partly as a votive ship and partly to commemorate the local men who gave their lives in the 1914-18 war. The design of the model was based on a well-known print of a Flemish carrack and was carried out with great care by Mr Leighton, whose son, incidentally made the commemorative model of HMS *Canterbury* for the Cathedral. The carracks were heavily built ships, among the first to have three masts, and were characterised by having distinctive overhanging forecastles. Such vessels traded between the continent and the Kentish ports during the fifteenth century. The model was beautifully detailed and included a large cargo port, a tub for unsalting meat as well as the circular fighting tops on the masts which were then essential even for a merchantman. Unfortunately the model was stolen early in 1993 and has yet to be found. Perhaps whoever has it now will at some time see that it is returned to an appropriate place.

Often models are not well documented and almost all the information

The conventional view of a hanging ship and a rare opportunity to see the deck details on this 50-gun model frigate. The Caledonia *was made by William Dunlop in the early years of the nineteenth century and is in St Cuthbert's Church, Saltcoats, Ardrossan. (Photos – Courtesy of Mr Phillip N. Thomas.)*

Cley-next-the-Sea on the Norfolk coast is home to this charming two-masted topsail schooner which possibly represents a ship that foundered there early in this century. (Photo – Courtesy of Col. F. A. Manning.]

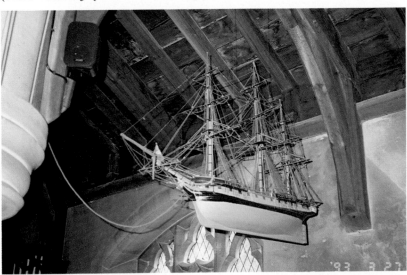

A modern votive model of the early nineteenth century frigate HMS Hotspur *which was made by Peter Clissold and presented to St Mary's Church, Hook-with-Warsash, Hampshire in 1973. (Photo – Courtesy of Mrs Catherine Parkes.)*

about them comes from oral traditions. This tends to apply to classic eighteenth and nineteenth century schooners, of varying ages, which have often been in their places of worship for as long as a century or so without any records surviving about their origins or prevenance. Sometimes parishes are fortunate in having dedicated people with the skills to research and to restore those that have been long neglected. When there are no recorded reasons for their presence in the churches they are generally considered votive models and they have been so classified here for convenience. There is one in the Lady Chapel in St Margaret's Parish Church, Cley-next-the-Sea in Norfolk. It is a delightful model of a two-masted top-sail schooner, measuring about 18 inches long, probably made in the early part of this century. As so often happens the parish terrier, in which the contents of the church may have been listed, is missing and there are no records other than the memories of local people. In this case a retired resident remembers it being in the church at least seventy years ago and a very elderly man recalled that traditionally it represented a ship that foundered off the coast early in the century and was thought to be a focus for prayers for those lost in the wreck. Where one might hope to find a name there is only a piece of printed paper, with the words Cley-next-the-Sea, glued on the stern.

The Parish Church of St Mary and St Leonard at Kinghorn in Fife is the possesor of a three hundred year old model of the warship HMS *Unicorn*. It is in the Sailor's Aisle which was added to the church in the seventeenth century. The model measures about two feet six inches long and has recently been put in a perspex case to protect it from deterioration. It is reputed to have been made by prisoners on the island of Inch Keith and presented to the Auld Kirk in Kinghorn about 1643. In a letter to *Country Life*, September 12th 1908, the then Minister the Revd A.H. M'Ilraith described it as 'A splendid model of the *Unicorn*, the flagship of Sir William Kirkaldy of Grange, who was sent with the Scotch fleet in pursuit of the Earl of Bothwell when, outlawed, he took to piracy off the Orkney Islands in 1567. Tradition has it that it was made by sailors who were with him in the expedition. It is still known as the *Unicorn* and is so named on the flag at the masthead.'

It should not be thought that votive offerings of such models only took place in the distant past. Although many were also made in the 1920s and 1930s immediately after the 1914-18 war the custom still continues. A very elegant modern example is the beautiful model of HMS *Hotspur* now in the church of St Mary's, Hook-with-Warsash, on the Hamble river in Hampshire. The vessel is a quarter of an inch to the foot scale model of a 36-gun frigate of 950 tons which was built between 1807 and 1810 at Mrs Parson's boatyard at Warsash. The model was made by Commander

Peter Clissold, sometime Master Mariner at the local School of Navigation, from the original drawings supplied by the National Maritime
Museum. It thus has historical significance and value as well as a little bit
of mystery. From ancient times it has been the practice of shipbuilders to
provide ritual hiding places in the hulls for 'good luck' coins, much as
coin-containing 'time capsules' are still put under foundation stones of
new buildings. Sometimes they were placed in the hole in the keel
extension that held the rudder pintle but more often they were hidden
under the mainmast. It was traditional for the coins to be minted in the
same year as the vessel was built. In the *Hotspur* Peter Clissold placed a
silver sixpence, minted in 1967, under his mainmast and also put into the
hold some fragments of timber from six historic ships. Started in 1966 it
took some seven years of his spare time to complete and became his own
votive offering to St Mary's.

Peter Clissold went to sea at a very early age and was a deeply religious
man. In later life he was an acknowledged authority on the naval memorials
in the churches in the Solent area. His daughter records that 'he remained
passionately interested in the sea and felt a seafarer's closeness to his
God'. It gave him great satisfaction when his model was received by the
Vicar on June 24th 1973. A nearby plaque records that it was given –

TO THE GLORY OF GOD
And in thankfulness for blessings received
on sea and on shore.

A more recent offering has been made in the Parish Church of
Liverpool, Our Lady and St Nicholas. In May 1993 the church was the
centre of the commemoration of the fiftieth anniversary of the Battle of
the Atlantic. During the year a new maritime chapel, St Mary of the
Quay, was dedicated and a fine votive model was hung from the oak
screen surrounding the chapel. The model is essentially a decorative one
based on a typical fifteenth century armed merchantman of the carrack
type. It has a well detailed hull, is fully rigged and has finely painted sails.
An anonymous donor, who had himself been a sailor, made and presented
it to the church in 1993. The chapel is also adorned with the late Arthur
Dooley's beautiful new bronze of St Mary of the Quay standing on the
prow of a boat. Both the bronze and the model celebrate the link between
the arduous and dangerous work of the seafarers and the divine world in a
way that is still relevant at the end of the twentieth century.

Another striking presentation of a votive ship took place, many miles
from the sea, in the church of St Mary the Virgin in Bletchingley, near
Redhill in Surrey, in the 1960s. It was in October 1961 that the world

Built and presented by an anonymous worshipper, this decorative model based on a fifteenth century carrack was installed in the chapel of St Mary of the Quay in Liverpool Parish Church during the summer of 1993. (Photo – Courtesy of The Revd Canon Nicholas Frayling.)

suddenly became aware of a tiny island, Tristan da Cunha in the South Atlantic, which had been devastated by a volcanic eruption of massive proportions. The island was rendered uninhabitable and as a result all the islanders, mostly fishermen and their wives and families, were evacuated to England where they remained for a year or so until it was possible for them to return home. During this time some of them were accommodated in an army camp near to Bletchingley and, when the time came for them to go back to Tristan da Cunha, they expressed their appreciation of the welcome and the care that they had been given by the villagers by making and presenting to the church a model of one of their characteristic open longboats.

The making of these models has long been a tradition on the island. There is a reference to them in 1928 when they are described and illustrated in one of Percival Marshall's books, 'Wonderful Models'. 'The inhabitants are only visited once a year by a British warship but, nevertheless, model making is practised there as is evidenced by the illustration representing two of their canvas sailing boats some 18 feet long of the type commonly used on the island. When it is remembered that the island is little more than an extinct [sic] volcano and that supplies ordered this year could not be received until a year or so later, the models must surely be accounted amongst the most wonderful of any in this book'.

Today the island is visited by mail boats some three times a year but otherwise little has changed for the 250 inhabitants. It was not recorded by whom the church model was made but through the kindness of one of the parishioners, Mrs Jean Kent, the author made contact with some of the present-day model makers on the island with a view to acquiring one of the open fishing boats for his collection. Communications are still difficult and it was over eight months before a model, virtually identical to the votive one in St Mary's, was received. It had been made by one of the pensioners on Tristan, Mr Walter Swain, who himself was one of the islanders who came to Britain so long ago. It is a true folk boat, made in the traditional way with love and care by one who was familiar with sailing the original. The hull is a simple wooden framework covered with painted canvas and it is equipped with oars, rowlocks, cleats and a working rudder. The rig is somewhat curious with a tiny headsail and a version of a gaff-rigged mainsail.

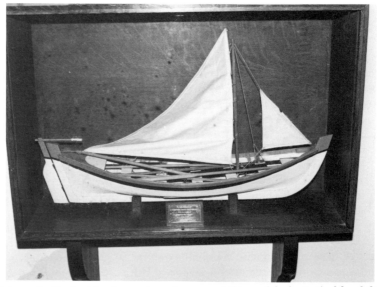

A Tristan da Cunha islander made and presented this model of a typical local fishing boat to Bletchingley Church, Surrey, in thankfulness for the kindness of the people there to him and his compatriates after the eruption of the Tristan volcano in 1961.

4

Missionary Ships and Lifeboats

From the beginnings of Christianity the Word was spread by missionaries on land and sea. For centuries seafarers themselves contributed to this. The very concept of 'ship' as having a symbolic meaning in the Christian faith was often carried by them from one civilization to another and it is understandable that potential converts would associate the message which the missionary brought with the means by which he arrived. In more recent times the Society for Promoting Christian Knowledge, which was established in London in 1698, was the first body in Britain to propose sending missionaries to the Americas. The Reverend Thomas Bray, a Church of England clergyman, conceived the idea of a society 'to promote Religion and Learning in the Plantations abroad and to propagate Christian Knowledge at home'. After a visit to Maryland he changed his original plans for a voluntary organisation to provide support for the Church in the colonies and in 1701 obtained a Royal Charter establishing the Society for the Propagation of the Gospel in Foreign Parts. The latter, now the U.S.P.G. and the S.P.C.K. thus have very closely related origins.

The first missionary for the Society for the Propagation of the Gospel was the Revd George Keith who set sail for the New World in 1701 in HMS *Centurion*, a three-masted man-of-war, to do a reconnaissance. On the voyage he inspired the ship's chaplain, the Revd John Talbot, to join him on his tour. Talbot was later to take charge of the parish of Burlington, New Jersey.

In 1951 as a part of their 250th anniversary celebrations the Society converted a fishing boat into a half-sized replica of the *Centurion* which undertook a triumphant missionary circumnavigation of the British Isles during the Festival of Britain celebrations. John Dixon, the U.S.P.G. Secretary at the time, supervised the conversion and skippered the vessel on its journey which was also continued during the following year. Missionaries from all over the world travelled on her and led a series of highly successful rallies in ports all round the coasts, including the Channel Islands. Many older members still remember the impact that the tour made.

At the same time numbers of collecting boxes were issued to churches and elsewhere which were decorated with models of the *Centurion*. The

In 1951 the Society for the Propagation of the Gospel converted a fishing boat into a half-size replica of their original missionary vessel Centurion *as part of the 250th anniversary celebrations of her first expedition to America. A twentieth century missionary cruise round the British Isles was a great success. (Photo – Courtesy of the U.S.P.G.)*

Miniature replicas of the Centurion *made from papier maché were used to ornament U.S.P.G. collecting boxes. Some are still in use in rural churches.*

models were very simple, made largely of papier maché, and were very attractive. Each flag represented a country where the Society works and when £1.00 had been collected a flag was put on the rigging. A *Centurion* model, minus its collecting box, remains in St Mary's Church, Purton in Wiltshire, with many flags still flying. A note alongside says that ultimately there were 25 flags on their model and that £20-16s-8d was raised by the catechism. Another, mounted on its collecting box, was found in Little Barrington Church in Gloucestershire and has recently been repaired. The Society has no record of who manufactured the models or how many were made. Only two or three are still in its possession, but even more than forty years after they were first issued it is quite possible that there are many more to be located. Any survivors are likely to be lying neglected in some corner of a vestry. They have now additional historical interest and it is to be hoped that any discovered will be restored and cherished.

The replica *Centurion* was owned and crewed by members of the Society; at the end of the tour she was laid up at Wivenhoe in Essex and later sold to a television company who used her in several programmes. For her last appearance she was masquerading as *The Golden Hind* when, in November 1987, she sank in a storm off the coast of Cornwall

In 1881 the Mission to Deep Sea Fishermen was formed by Ebenezer Mather in London to minister to the Thames fishing community. The Mission developed rapidly and soon extended its influence to the North Sea fishing fleet. Its first ship was a 56 ton yawl-rigged smack which was based at Yarmouth. This was the Mission Ship *Ensign*, later renamed *Thomas Gray*. Within ten years eight ships were in commission and their sphere of influence extended to the fleets fishing off Newfoundland. They were easily identified with their white sails, enormous light blue flags and the legends painted on their prows 'Preach the Word: Heal the Sick'. The Mission was (and is) Non-Denominational and from the beginning was concerned to bring material comfort and healing as well as spiritual enlightenment to the fishing communities.

Activities continued little changed until, after World War II the ships were sold and the Mission concentrated on developing its shore Institutes where there was need, from Lerwick to Newlyn. Each has a room that is used as a chapel and in many there have been model ships mainly used as decoration. At the Mallaig Centre on the west coast of Scotland are four ship models, three of which are typical of some of the vessels the present-day fishermen crew. There is the motor fishing vessel *Aquilla*, of which nothing seems to be known and two others, MFV *Solan* and MFV *Minch Harvester*. These are locally made models commissioned by the boats' owners and it is gratifying that they have this feeling for their vessels.

They are on permanent loan to the Mission and contribute greatly to the atmosphere of the place. The fourth vessel is a model of the *PS Comet*, the first sea going paddle steamer which was for many years at the Oban Centre before being transferred to Mallaig when the latter closed.

The London Missionary Society still uses ships and one of them is both commemorated, and in part supported, by a church model. This is at present in Emmanuel Church, Ilfracombe and is the centrepiece of a monthly ceremony for the children. The vessel is the *John Williams VII*, the inheritor of a long line of ships bearing this name which have belonged to the London Missionary Society since the middle of the nineteenth century.

John Williams was born in 1796 and as a young man developed a range of practical skills which he proposed to use to help him as a missionary. When he was only twenty he joined the newly formed London Missionary Society and, in 1816, sailed with his wife Mary to the South Sea Islands. On the journey he learned all he could about the ship, its construction,

This somewhat naive waterline model of the London Missionary Society's ship John Williams VII *is the focus of a monthly collection ceremony for the children of Emmanuel Church, Ilfracombe. It stands alongside the pulpit and has masthead and navigation lamps which are switched on during the service.*

the techniques of sailing it and something about the rules of navigation. When he arrived he sought to teach the islanders as many practical skills as possible with a view to building some sort of boat with which to travel between the host of tiny islands. The somewhat surprising result was *The Messenger of Peace*, a vessel which he used for his work among the islanders for some five years. This was later replaced with another from England which continued in use until, in 1843, John Williams was murdered by some of the people he had come out to help.

This tragedy made such a deep impression on members of the Congregational Churches that they set about raising funds to build a ship, the *John Williams I*, in his memory. It was launched in 1843 and a substantial part of the money was raised by the children who continued to collect funds for its maintenance. This tradition has continued and a total of six missionary ships had been built and maintained before the present, the seventh, was launched in 1962.

John Williams VII was named at Tower Pier, London in November 1962 by H.R.H Princess Margaret. Members of the Junior Church in Ilfracombe had always made a significant contribution to the funds and latterly, in the days before decimal coinage, they collected the 'ship' halfpennies for the cause. To encourage this a local friend of the church, Mr Ireland, made a waterline model of the *John Williams VII* which he presented to the Junior Church. Over the years the Congregational Church became the United Reformed and, in 1987, joined with the Methodist Church in Ilfracombe to form the present United Church.

The model has gone with them and is now mounted on a stand near the pulpit in Emmanuel Church. It has a masthead light that is switched on at the monthly ceremony at which the children make their offerings. Elsewhere there are pictures, presented by the London Missionary Society, of two of the earlier vessels, number five, launched in 1930 and number six commissioned in 1948.

The spiritual concerns of the missionary societies have their temporal counterparts in the lifeboat service. It was not until the end of the eighteenth century that serious attempts were made to design and build special pulling boats for rescuing the shipwrecked. The first consideration was to reduce the tendency to capsize or to sink in heavy seas. The Royal National Lifeboat Institution, established in 1824, has used model boats for many years as a focus for fund raising, the famous orange lifeboat collecting boxes having been first issued in the 1960s. The blue and white models follwed and today there are 'rocking' boats which were introduced in the late 1980s. They are occasionally displayed for special services in churches but most R.N.L.I. models appear to be in their own lifeboat stations or in maritime museums.

In the eighteenth century the Tyne was a particularly difficult river to enter and many ships came to grief on the neighbouring rocks. As a result of one tragedy, when the merchant ship *Adventure* was wrecked on the Herd Sands, a local committee was set up to commission a boat that would be capable of putting to sea in difficult conditions to save life. William Wouldhave, a local housepainter of an inventive turn of mind, who made clocks and musical instruments among other things, submitted a design called a Life-Boat which was built for £91 and launched in 1790. It was based on the local cobles, boats with fine seakeeping qualities. Although not wholly satisfactory this first lifeboat nevertheless survived

A drawing of a contemporary model of one of the first lifeboats made in 1790 by William Wouldhave which hangs in his parish church, St Hilda's, South Shields.

for forty years and helped to rescue many lives. Unfortunately for Wouldhave, ten years later another local man, Henry Greathead, made improvements to the boat and, with influential backing from the Duke of Northumberland among others, submitted his design to the Society for the Encouragement of Arts, Manufactures and Commerce in London for a premium. In 1802 it was recorded that 'The Gold Medal and Fifty Guineas were this Sesson [sic] voted as a Bounty to Mr Henry Greathead, of South Shields, for a boat of a peculiar construction, named a Life-Boat, in consequence of the lives of many persons shipwrecked having been preserved by it.'

There seems little doubt that Greathead copied the Wouldhave design. It had long been the practice to 'girdle' ships by fastening additional timbers round the waterline to increase stability. Wouldhave improved this by using cork both inside and out to increase buoyancy and his boat was virtually unsinkable. Greathead's marginal improvement was achieved by cambering the keel to make it more manoeuverable. He undoubtedly succeeded in popularising and selling his lifeboats. By the time the National Institution for the Preservation of Life from Shipwreck (today the RNLI) was formed in 1824 Greathead lifeboats were in use in many coastal towns, including Scarborough, Lowestoft, Montrose, St Andrews and Ramsgate as well as Liverpool and Dublin. One was also sent as far afield as Oporto but, despite all this, Greathead had become bankrupt by 1825.

Although the invention of the lifeboat is popularly ascribed to Greathead it is William Wouldhave who is rightly honoured in South Shields, where he was for many years the parish clerk. He died in 1821 and is buried in St Hilda's (or St Hild's), the parish church of South Shields and a model of his lifeboat has reputedly hung in the main aisle since 1805. It is made of wood, painted to look like bronze, and has a crew of twelve, which was probably added later. Alongside is a fine chandelier and it is thought that the model originally hung above this, transfixed through its middle by the chandelier support. It is still possible to see where the hole in the bottom of the boat has been filled in.

The model is much like the drawings of Greathead's boat which were published in the Transactions of the Society of Arts. He donated a model, made to the scale of one inch to the foot, to the Society but it has since been lost. It has been suggested that the model in St Hilda's might in fact have been made by Stephen Laverick, one of Greathead's apprentices in 1802, but this is probably the tin model which is in the Museum. The ancient rivalry between the two men might well justify further study.

There is a simple model in the Parish Church of St Peter in Folkestone but perhaps the most interesting one is in the parish church of St Edmund in the quiet seaside resort of Southwold. This is one of the magnificent fifteenth century Perpendicular churches in East Suffolk. It has a windvane in the form of an East Coast sailing drifter on the tower and a very much older model of a lifeboat in the nave. The story of the lifeboat and its model, spanning over one hundred years, is one of gratitude for the achievements of the lifeboat crews and an acknowledgement of the craft skills of the local people. The first Southwold lifeboat, propelled by sail and oars, was the *Alfred Corrie*, launched in 1893. She was a highly successful craft and for the next twenty years took part in innumerable rescues without the loss of any of her crew. On her replace-

This model of the Alfred Corrie, *launched in 1893, hangs in St Peter's, Southwold as a memento of the first lifeboat to be stationed there. It has been there since 1913 when the original boat was replaced. (Photo – Courtesy of Mrs Shirley Cordeaux).*

ment in 1913 the then town clerk, Mr Ernest Read Cooper, secured a faculty for a model to be suspended from the roof of the church at the west end of the north aisle as a token of gratitude for the saftey of the lifeboatmen whilst the *Alfred Corrie* was in service.

The model is marked *Southwold No 1* because there were at some time two lifeboats in commision. This extract from the *East Anglian Daily Times*, dated March 25th 1913 records the dedication service.

'This Easter was notable for the addition of a model of a lifeboat at present stationed at Southwold but which will shortly be replaced. The model was executed by Mr J. May, one of the crew of the lifeboat, and brother of the coxwain, Mr S. May; it is built to a scale of three-quarters of an inch to the foot. She is complete in every part and is a beautiful piece of work. The model was made to the order of Mr E.R. Cooper, the secretary of the Southwold branch of the Royal National Lifeboat Institution, and was presented to the church as a memorial to the good work the boat and her crew have accomplished in life-saving.

The model is suspended fron the roof of the north side of the church and bears the following inscription, "Dedicated to the Eternal Father in gratitude for the safety of the *Alfred Corrie* lifeboat during twenty years of service at Southwold, by Ernest R. Cooper, lifeboat secretary 1893 – Easter 1913."'

She survived the First World War but thirty years later, on the 15th of May 1943, the church suffered severly in an air raid. The model fell to the ground and was badly damaged. The Parish Magazine for August 1943 records that the *Alfred Corrie* was repaired 'thanks to the skill and craftmanship of Mr Deal and Mr Taylor who repainted the craft and put it back in its place in the north aisle without a trace of the damage showing'. She is still there today, her name somewhat crudely painted as befits a lovingly built sailor-made model, with the inscription still visible above the starboard bilge keel.

The Golden Hind *is one of our most popular historic ships and during the 1920s and 1930s companies such as Bassett-Lowke Ltd and Hobbies Ltd sold drawings and parcels of wood and other materials from which attractive models could be made. Early outfits such as these could have formed the bases of some of the church models.*

5

Historic Ships Commemorated

Lord Nelson's HMS *Victory* and the fast clipper ship *Cutty Sark* are among those ships with famous names, known in every household, which bring to mind our long naval and mercantile marine history. Most of us can name others which have made their mark upon our heritage and culture – HMS *Bounty*, which had a famous mutiny, HMS *Beagle*, the research vessel which prompted Charles Darwin to formulate his challenging theory of evolution, as well as HMS *Golden Hind* and *The Mayflower*

It is therefore a little surprising that few of these are commemorated in places of worship. There is an undistinguished model of the hull of the *Victory* made from oak and copper from the original vessel in St Ann's Church on the naval base at Portsmouth. The present church was opened in 1786. It was severely damaged by enemy bombs in 1941 and has now been restored. The model was made in 1963 by coppersmith and joiner apprentices of the Constructive Department at Portsmouth. Another *Victory* is a damaged one which is fortuitously part of an eclectic collection of models in All Hallows-by-the-Tower in London. It would seem that it is those ships having a very localised appeal which are of the greatest interest to the congregations. As might be expected the *Mayflower* is commemorated in Boston, Lincolnshire and also, a little curiously, in Babworth in Nottinghamshire.

The exploits and achievements of Sir Francis Drake are part of our folklore and he and the famous *Golden Hind* are celebrated in more than one church. A model of his later flagship the *Bonaventure* is the symbolic ship in Painswick Parish Church (See page 6) but the *Golden Hind* was the vessel in which he made the first circumnavigation of the world in 1577 – 1581. It was as the *Pelican* that she set sail, under Drake's command, from Plymouth in November 1577, bound for Egypt. The ship was quite small, something between a merchant vessel and a warship, and probably mounted eighteen cannon. A convoy of five vessels started out but only the *Golden Hind* returned. The object of the voyage was ostensibly to explore the south-west passage to Asia across the Pacific. Bringing back treasure, by plundering any newly discovered countries and taking such 'prize' ships on the way as were unfortunate enough to cross Drake's path, provided the financial incentive for the adventure.

Privateering was the word used to describe these activities but piracy would be as appropriate. When off the coast of Africa Drake took a prize and put on board a few men under a junior officer. They promptly made off with it, which Drake regarded as mutiny, and he also considered his own ship and its company disgraced by the affair. For this reason he changed her name and it was as the *Golden Hind* that she continued the voyage to Brazil, along the South American coast before returning to Deptford via Cape Horn and the Cape of Good Hope with a vast cargo of treasure.

Queen Elizabeth I knighted Drake on board the *Golden Hind* at Deptford in 1581 and ordered that the vessel be preserved. Some steps were taken tu do this but she only lasted for a few more years before rotting away. However, to commemorate the 400th anniversary of Drake's voyage a full-sized replica was built at Appledore in Devonshire. She was greeted by a salute from 14 cannons when she sailed into Plymouth Sound on a celebration visit in 1993, by which time it had become fashionable to spell her name *Golden Hinde*.

Francis Drake's father was one time chaplain at the Royal Dockyard, Chatham and the young Drake learned to sail in the surrounding waters during his boyhood. To commemorate his association with the Dockyard a model of the *Golden Hind* was presented to the Chapel in October 1927 as part of the 300th anniversary celebrations of her departure (as the *Pelican*) from Plymouth. It was made by Mr J.J. Hardman in the Dockyard and was the gift of Rear-Admiral C.P. Beatty-Pownall. At the ceremony he said 'I unveil this ship's model to the Glory of God and in recollection that this Church is used by those who build ships and by those who serve in them'.

When the third jubilee of the 1808 opening of the Dockyard Chapel was celebrated in 1958 the model was completely re-rigged and the flags arranged to fly correctly. She flies the Cross of St George at the mizzen mast, a standard at the main with French quarterings and the flag of Queen Elizabeth I flies at the foremast. The model still hangs in front of the High Altar in the Chapel which is now in the care of the Chatham Historic Dockyard Trust and open to the public.

Before describing other models of the *Golden Hind* there is an example of a well-known but very specialised type of ship model in the chapel at Chatham. This is the bone Napoleonic prisoner-of-war model which is on the left of the doorway when you go in. Such models are quite rare and they seldom appear in churches. It is there to remind us of the prisoners, over 120,000 of them between 1794 and 1815, who were accommodated, first in ships and later in camps and who made exquisite model ships from beef and mutton bones. They were allowed to sell these to supplement

A rare church model of HMS Victory, *damaged on the starboard side, is among the outstanding collection of models in All Hallows-by-the-Tower in London.*

The ship's bell from HMS Canterbury, in commission from 1916 to 1933, accompanies a model of the 1744 ship of the same name in Canterbury Cathedral. Both were dedicated in 1933. (Photo – Courtesy of Canterbury Cathedral.)

their meagre rations – presumably they bought more beef and mutton – and today are very much sought after by collectors. There are 36 examples in the Chichester Collection at Arlington Court in Devonshire (See page 19) which is perhaps the most representative collection in Britain.

Another fine model of the *Golden Hind*, fully rigged, hangs in the centre of the nave of the Church of St Nicholas in the naval base HMS *Drake* in Devonport. The foundation stone of the church was laid in 1905 but the model, which was made by some naval ratings on the base, is of later date and celebrates Drake's association with Plymouth.

A model and other Drake memorabilia are preserved in Buckland Abbey, Devonshire, which is now owned by the National Trust, in recognition of the family connections with the Abbey. The Cistercian Abbey, built in 1278, was turned into a house after the Reformation, and was sold by the Crown to Sir Richard Grenville, the hero of the *Revenge*, in 1541. Unusually he incorporated the monastic church and its tower into the house. It was later bought by Sir Francis in 1581 just after he was knighted and remained in the possession of his descendents until it was acquired by the National Trust in 1948. The house is in part a naval museum with both Grenville and Drake relics, including Drake's famous drum. The model of the *Golden Hind*, beautifully rigged with sails set, is in a glass case. Yet another model, reputedly over three hundred years old, is preserved in the Mariners' Chapel in All Hallows-by-the-Tower in London.

The seventeenth century was a time of profound and widespread religious conflict resulting in much persecution of those, such as the Quakers, the Puritans and the Separatists, who would not conform to the requirements of the state church. Among these were the Pilgrim Fathers who sailed for America in the *Mayflower* and founded the town of Boston in Massachusetts. One of the results of the increasing interest in the Pilgrim Fathers has been the setting up of the Mayflower Trail in north Nottinghamshire to encourage visitors to explore some of the villages and churches associated with the early leaders of the Separatist movement. One of these is the village of Babworth a few miles from Retford where, from 1586 to 1605, the parson was Richard Clyfton. He became a non-conformist for which he was deprived of his living, and two of his friends, William Brewster and William Bradford, later sailed on the *Mayflower*.

In 1970, 350 years after the sailing of the *Mayflower* for the New World in 1620, the event was celebrated at All Saints' Church, Babworth by the acquisition of a model of the ship. Just to emphasize that there is nothing stereotyped about commemorative ship models this one was made, perhaps as an act of expiation and, hopefully, to the glory of God, by some of the prisoners at nearby Ranby Prison. They used hundreds of

Large numbers of model ships were made from bones by French prisoners of war early in the nineteenth century. There is a good example on the left of the doorway to the chapel in the Royal Dockyard, Chatham. (Photo – Courtesy of Sotheby's Ltd.)

matchsticks in its construction. The appearance of the original vessel is notoriously uncertain and the model was made from the plans produced for the replica *Mayflower II*.

Some uncertainty also extends to the model, reputed to be of the *Mayflower*, which is in St Botolph's Parish Church at Boston in Lincolnshire. There are inconsistencies in the history of this particular model and the following information about it owes much to the careful research done by Mr John Orange, the curator of the church records and library. The ship is about 28 inches long and the same height. It is a carefully made and well detailed piece of work possibly made in 1920 to celebrate the 300th anniversary of the sailing of the *Mayflower*. Most models are made of wood but this one is fashioned from sheet copper with copper wire for standing and running rigging, ratlines and coiled ropes on deck. Copper is a delightfully malleable metal to work and does not corrode. The *Golden Barque* in Portsmouth Cathedral (See page 12) is the only other copper model so far found and that, of course, was for centuries in the open air as a windvane. St Botolph's model was never intended as a windvane. It was made for an unknown customer by a local sheet metal company which no longer exists; P. Waples & Son of Vauxhall Works.

There are few records of its provenance and it may have been made for the Guildhall and later loaned to the church. About fifteen years ago it seems to have been 'borrowed' for a short time before being returned to the church, after which it was put in its present glass case. Though it is not equipped with guns it is more like a warship than a merchant vessel and this has led Mr Orange to doubt whether it was ever intended to represent the *Mayflower*, though it conforms to the popular notion of what she looked like. It must be said, of course, that in fact she never even visited Boston; it was from Plymouth that she sailed to the New World in 1620. The popular misconception arose because meetings of the Separatists were held in Boston and the ring leaders, William Bradford and William Brewster, were for a time imprisoned there before they sailed illegally to the Netherlands in 1607. The association was sealed by their adoption of the name of Boston for their settlement in Massachusetts.

The church of Christ the King in the seaside village of Coatham on the outskirts of Redcar in Cleveland has a model of the *Santa Maria*. She was, of course, Christopher Columbus's tiny flagship in which he made his epic voyage of discovery. The model was found some years ago, in a distressed condition, by John Crowther, a lay reader. Being a skilled model maker he re-rigged and restored it in 1976. The hull is about 2 feet long and has been carved from a solid block of yellow pine. The stern gallery and some of the detailing is rather heavy and this suggests that it was originally a sailor's model, perhaps made as a latter day tribute to the skills of the early navigators. It is a matter of some satisfaction that it has been brought back to the church where it is placed on the pulpit as a focus for the address on 'Sea Sunday'.

In Lincoln Cathedral a vessel, a man and his achievements are celebrated. Although the Seaman's Chapel, dedicated to St Andrew, was restored in 1923 it was not until 1950 that steps were taken to install an appropriate model ship. Late in the eighteenth century and in the early part of the nineteenth there was a great increase in geographical curiosity about the world. In 1770 Captain Cook had discovered Australia but it was not until some thirty years later that Captain Matthew Flinders (1774–1814), the Lincolnshire born explorer, was sent by the newly formed Admiralty Hydrographic Department to map and chart the Australian coastline. His vessel, a converted Whitby collier, was named HMS *Investigator* and since it was thought to be a suitable prototype a model was commissioned from Leslie Wilcox, of Lincoln's Inn. It was finished in March 1950. HMS *Investigator* was only about 100 feet long and the model, beautifully detailed, measures some four feet overall. While Captain Flinders had been held a Napoleonic prisoner of war in Mauritius he had written a paper for the Royal Society on deviations in the compass which resulted in a widely used correction device known as a Flinders Bar.

At the end of World War II when the Festival of Britain was reflecting a new feeling of national pride, on June 2nd 1951, there was a Seamen's Service of Remembrance and Dedication in Lincoln Cathedral attended by Admiral-of-the-Fleet Lord Tovey and a host of local dignitaries. The Bishop of Willesdan, formerly Chaplain of HMS *Howe* preached and, referring to the model, said, 'The furnishings of the Chapel are given in memory of all seafaring men, in whatever kind of ship, who fought for a Christian world, whether they knew it or not'.

The 1930s saw the donation of an appropriate ship model to Canterbury Cathedral. In 1935 there is an account in the magazine *Ships and Ship Models* of the work of Mr J.W. Leighton of Fordwich who built a 1-60th scale model, 4 feet 6 inches long, of the 1744 60-gun ship HMS *Canterbury*. Mr Leighton was the son of the maker of the model carrack which hung until recently in Fordwich Church (See page 24). It was presented to the Cathedral by Mrs Levi of Folkestone in memory of Capt G.R.L. Edwardes, R.N. who had commanded the later *Canterbury* which was in commission between 1916 and 1933. A subtle touch, which highlights the connection between the model and its prototype, is that the hull of the model is carved from a piece of teak taken from the deck of the *Canterbury* when she was broken up. The ship's bell was already in the Cathedral and the model was placed on the top of the frame supporting it when it was dedicated on November 10th 1935.

Photographs of Mr Leighton working on the model, and of its installation in the Cathedral, appear in the magazine *Ships and Ship Models*. At this time it was complete with standing rigging but with no sails. A later postcard showed it still on its frame but with yards and sails set. Today the model complete with sails, together with the bell, is mounted on brackets on a pillar in St Michael's Chapel in the South West Transept, known as the Warriors' Chapel. The care and maintenance of the model is in the hands of the curators at the National Maritime Museum, Greenwich. Some time in the past fifty years it has been equipped with sails thus making it a more spectacular model. This was presumably done by the museum staff.

The model of HMS *Canterbury* is the focus for a daily ceremony taking place at 11am which includes prayers for peace and the remembrance of those who have died in warfare, not only the seafarers. A page is turned in the Memorial books of the local regiment.

Another cathedral warship, somewhat earlier, is HMS *Sussex* which is to be found in Chichester Cathedral. Hanging from the archway leading from the nave to the Chapel of St Michael, called the Sailors' Chapel, is a modern model of the first HMS *Sussex*, a 42-gun warship which was built at Deptford in 1652. The Chapel was dedicated as a memorial to the men of Sussex who lost their lives in the second World War. The model is suspended high up and appears to be about 2 feet long. It was made by Mr J. Glossop, an official Admiralty modelmaker, specially for the dedication of the Chapel in 1956.

Not far away, set in deep countryside, is the parish church of the tiny village of Boldre in the New Forest. It is something of a surprise to find that St John's contains many memorials to the officers and men of HMS *Hood*. The loss of the *Hood* was one of the great naval tragedies of the last war. Launched in 1923 she was the pride of the British navy. In the early stages of the battle of the Atlantic she came under fire from the German

Chichester Cathedral's Sailors' Chapel, dedicated to St Michael, has this modern model of the first HMS Sussex, *launched in 1652, to commemorate the sailors who lost their lives in the Second World War.*

battleship *Bismark* at the end of May 1941. The terse communiqué from the German High Command, dated Sunday May 25th, stated 'After a short but intense engagement the battleship *Bismark* sank the British battlecruiser *Hood*, the largest ship in the British navy.' Her dramatic end came when a shell struck her magazine. Of her complement of 1341 officers and men only three survived.

Perhaps because Vice-Admiral L.E. Holland was a regular worshipper at Boldre, St John's has been chosen to commemorate those who lost their lives. The memorials include a Book of Remembrance and two models of the *Hood*. One was presented in 1955 and the other, probably sailor made with its sombre Admiralty grey paint, was given in 1990 on the occasion of the annual memorial service. There is little satisfaction to be gained from a subsequent communiqué from the Germans, issued three days after the *Hood* had been blown up, 'May 27th *Bismark* sunk by torpedoes launched by enemy torpedo aircraft.'

With some relief one turns from warships to a famous commercial vessel which is commemorated by a fine model in St Mary's Cathedral, Edinburgh. This is the tea clipper *Ariel*, one of the last of a noted fleet of beautiful, fast sailing ships engaged in the China tea trade in the middle of last century. The model has been here for at least fifty years since the Cathedral became a member of the Missions to Seamen for which an annual collection is made. The ship was built for Shaw and Moxton in Robert Steele and Company's yard at Greenock and launched on the 29th of June 1865. An early example of composite construction, she had iron frames clad with teak planking as well as iron masts. With an overall length of 197 feet and a beam of 33 feet she was a finely designed vessel which could achieve a speed of 16 knots in good conditions. Built four years before the more famous *Cutty Sark* she is of broadly similar design and is one of few ships that made the voyage to Hong Kong in under 100 days. Authorities who have compared the performances of the clipper ships usually award first place to *Ariel* followed by *Cutty Sark*. Whilst the latter still survives, *Ariel* only lasted for seven years; she left London for Sydney in January 1872 and was never heard of again, presumably succumbing to high seas and contrary winds in the South Atlantic.

It is appropriate that *Ariel* should be commemorated in Scotland's capital city. Lesser trading vessels and hard working fishing boats, often those which have suffered disaster, are most frequently celebrated in our smaller coastal churches and chapels. Many of these models were sailor built and have an indefinable magic born partly of their age and partly of their associations.

6

Trading Ships and Fishing Boats

Since early man first dug out a tree trunk to make a canoe, or bound reeds together to form a raft, boats have been used for fishing and the transport of goods. The building and sailing of boats have been the main preoccupations of generations of coastal communities; hence trading and fishing boats are those most frequently celebrated in their churches and chapels.

Although fish stocks have declined over the years there are still small fishing fleets around our coasts. Hastings, in Sussex, is the home of one of them. The old fishermen's church of St Nicholas still stands alongside the unique net drying and storage sheds at Rock-a-Nore at the eastern end of the town. When the church was built in 1854 about one hundred and fifty boats supported the population of the Old Town. The church is now a tiny maritime museum and among its treasures is the last of the sailing luggers, the *Enterprise*, built at Rock-a-Nore in 1909. When the church was converted in 1956 a breach had to be made in the wall for the *Enterprise* to be hauled in. She is very much a 'church ship', though not a votive model. An annual harvest festival is conducted by the Rector of the Old Town Churches who gives the address from the deck of the lugger. The text is always from Luke Ch.5 v.3, 'And He sat down and taught the people out of the ship'. A memorial window, showing one of the fishing luggers off the coast, is dedicated 'To the Glory of God, and in memory of all fishermen of Hastings who lost their lives at sea'.

For centuries the east coast fishing communities were heavily dependent on the annual migration of the herring and the mackerel from Scotland to the south coast. The days when huge fleets of steam and sailing drifters and trawlers followed them round have now gone but there are many memorials to them still to be found.

Most church models are some three or four feet long, occasionally up to about seven feet. In St Peter's Episcopal Church in Fraserburgh in Scotland is a vessel which, on first aquaintance, might be mistaken for a full-sized one, and indeed is fully capable of being sailed in calm seas. It is a replica of a local two-masted line fishing vessel which measures fifteen feet long, or half the size of the Hastings *Enterprise*. She has a respectable antiquity and has already outlived her first home. Made by the Aberdeen boatbuilder James Cordiner at the turn of the century she had hung, fully rigged with sails, from the roof of another St Peter's, in Torry, Aberdeen until 1983. The church was then closed as a place of worship and converted to a community hall while the massive model boat was found a new home in Fraserburgh. She bears the name *Ss Peter and Andrew* and the number A 153. The 'A' is the Aberdeen registration letter and the 153 refers to the number of fish that the disciples Peter and Andrew caught in the Sea of Galilee (St John Chapter 21 v.11).

We have already noted Capt Marr's model frigate in St Monan's church in Fife. (See page 22) There is, however, another model which was presented to the church in 1992. This is of a coastal fishing boat built locally in the East Neuk in 1908. It hangs under the North Archway in the nave. Another locally made model, this time of a traditional north-east coast fishing boat is in St Ebba's church in Eyemouth, Berwickshire. This was given to the church by Sir Christopher Furness who was a churchwarden there for many years. It was Sir Christopher who gave the model of the *Vale of Pickering* to York Minster. (See page 9)

We are reminded of the great days of the Tyne Tees area by the phrase 'taking coals to Newcastle' as an expression of futile endeavour. *Nora* is a model resembling one of Captain Cook's colliers now preserved in Christ Church, North Shields together with a West Indiaman named *Faithful Star*. In the 1950s a mariners' chapel, dedicated to St Nicholas, was created in the church by screening off the old organ chamber in the chancel. The two models are displayed on top of the screen. There is no record of when they were built but it is thought that both of them were originally builder's models. They were in a dilapidated condition and in 1952 they were re-rigged by a local parishioner, Mr Tom Bulman, who was a retired River Tyne police inspector and a talented model shipbuilder.

Further down the east coast there is an interesting model of a modern fishing vessel. This is in St Paul and St John's United Reformed Church in South Shields. It is a large model, probably to a scale of 1/8th inch to one foot, of the whaling factory ship *Southern Venturer*, registered at Leith. The case in which it is housed measures seven feet long. The model was probably made by a member of the staff of the Middle Docks and was presented in 1961 by one of the church members, Mr McMiniagle, who was the managing director of the Docks.

The 14,493-ton *Southern Venturer* was built on the Tees in 1945 and operated in the Antarctic. Every year she came back for a re-fit in the Middle Docks and became a well-loved local vessel. The economics of whaling became difficult and in 1962, to local dismay, she was sold to a Japanese firm who only bought her for the whaling quota she carried.

Faithful Star, *a nineteenth century West Indiaman some four feet long with her companion, the collier* Nora *in front of the 1962 'Lifeboat' window in the Mariners' Chapel in Christ Church, North Shields. (Photos – Courtesy of Mr M. Scott.)*

Neither she nor her sister ship, the *Southern Harvester*, ever worked again since the Japanese transferred the quotas to their own factory ships. It is gratifying that at least one of these ships should be remembered, and commemorated in model form, in a prominent place of worship on the Tyne.

All Saint's at Ingleby Arncliffe in North Yorkshire is a beautiful Regency church with many interesting features including a 3-decker pulpit, box pews and a splendid view of the moors through the plain glass windows. There is also a very large model of a Norwegian schooner, possibly dating from the late nineteenth century, though it is not known when the model was made. It was presented by the then vicar's warden, Miss Katherine Cooper-Abbs. She was very proud of her Norwegian ancestry which included shipping magnates who had been engaged in the trade between Teeside and the Scandinavian ports. It was to celebrate this that she donated to her church the magnificent model merchant ship over seven feet long and three feet high. Memories are short and there have been many changes in the past thirty years but it is thought that the model was presented when the church was restored in 1961. At this time it hung from the ceiling in the centre of the nave in accord with Norgegian tradition. However, it was felt that it obscured the view of the altar and

This modern factory whaling ship, the Southern Venturer, *is a somewhat unromantic reminder of the (recent) past prosperity of South Shields. It is in St Paul and St John's United Reformed Church in the Town. (Photo – Courtesy of Mr H. Gibson.)*

the east window and in 1989 it was moved to its present position above the West door. Sadly, Miss Cooper-Abbs was drowned in 1972 whilst taking part in a sponsored swim in aid of church funds.

The two adjacent fishing villages of Staithes and Hinderwell in Cleveland celebrate their local craft in their parish churches. Each has a model of a coble, one is in St Peter's, Staithes, the other is on a window ledge in St Hilda's, Hinderwell. In addition, St Peter's also uses another as a collecting box. The Oxford English Dictionary has a comprehensive but succinct description of the coble, 'A sea fishing-boat with a flat bottom, square stern and a rudder extending four or five feet below the bottom, rowed with three pairs of oars and furnished with a lug sail; used chiefly on the north east coast of England'. The models have been carved from the solid and are complete with masts, yards, tillers and oars. They are thought to have been made by one of the parishioners, the late Mr Metcalf. There are other models which are cherished in the homes of some of the village families and there is a local superstition that the models must always be kept so that they point out to sea.

An earlier memorial to fishermen is in St Margaret's Parish Church, Lowestoft. A splendid wall panel has a glass case set into it containing a beautifully detailed waterline model of a typical steam drifter. She bears

Lowestoft's fine waterline model of the 1909 steam drifter LT 762 is confusingly named Lily *on the prow and* Hilda Maud *on the stern. (Photo – Courtesy of Mr Reg Snell.)*

the Lowestoft registration number LT 762 but the name on the prow, *Lily* does not correspond with the name on the stern, *Hilda Maud*. Perhaps she is intended to represent two vessels. The prototype was probably built by Richards Ironworks, Lowestoft, and the model, whose maker is unknown, dates from about 1909 when the monument was set up. The boat is flanked by two pictures of drifters set in lifebelt frames and the carved inscription underneath reads –

'To the glory of God and in memory of those fishermen
from this coast who have lost their lives at sea while
in pursuit of their calling this faithful record is
dedicated AD. M.C.M.I.X.'

The Sailors' and Fishermen's Bethel at Battery Green, Lowestoft has a memorial, dedicated in 1955, to the memory of local seafarers lost at sea. This includes a scale model of the bows and wheelhouse of a steam drifter which fits onto the communion rail so that the central pulpit becomes the Bridge.

Our journey down the east coast takes us past Felixtowe and Harwich into the Thames estuary. Until very recently London's dockland was the largest and the busiest in Britain. Vast numbers of ships berthed in the Pool of London where commercial activity extended up to London Bridge. Millions of tons of merchandise were handled annually. The Billingsgate fish market was legendary. Shipping was under the control of the Port of London Authority whose jurisdiction extended from Teddington to the Nore lightship. The PLA's headquarters and the Custom House are on the north bank of the river near to Tower Bridge and in the parish of All Hallows -by-the-Tower. For generations those concerned with London' s commercial enterprises have been among the worshippers at this and other City churches.

The links have been very close and it would seem appropriate that these would be commemorated in a number of churches by ship models. However, it is interesting that almost all of them, ten in number, are concentrated in All Hallows-by-the-Tower. Founded four hundred years before the Tower of London, All Hallows has been a centre of worship ever since and its history is the history of the City of London. It survived the Great Fire of London in 1666 and Samuel Pepys climbed its tower to describe the devastation. However, it was severely damaged by German bombs in 1940 and much of the present structure has been rebuilt. Today it is an island of tranquility in London's traffic and it is also the mother church of the Toc H movement.

The close ties with the Thames are celebrated in the Mariners' Chapel

The outstanding collection of models in All Hallows-by-the-Tower reflects its historical associations with the Port of London and its ancient institutions. Among the models installed or re-instated after the bombing in 1940 this Santa Maria *may be the earliest.*

in which the wooden screen commemorates the links with the Port of London Authority. There is a crucifix made of wood that came from the *Cutty Sark* and the ivory figure is reputed to have come from the captain's cabin of the flagship of the Spanish Armada. A number of people have recollections of ship models in the church during the 1930s but there are few details of them. It is uncertain whether they were removed before the war or survived the bombing. There seems to be little recorded about many of the models and oral tradition has to be relied upon to supplement the information available from examining them.

The only one that is known to have been in the church before the war is the model of the *Golden Hind* which is on a window ledge in front of a vivid stained glass window that makes photography very difficult. When staff from the National Maritime Museum at Greenwich examined the model they thought that it was probably made during the sixteenth century. Above the gallery door, fixed to the wall, is a model of the *Santa Maria*. There seems to be nothing known either about the model or its reason for being there. Next to this is an elaborate model of the *Victory* which was apparently the subject of an attempted burglary some years ago as a result of which the starboard side was badly damaged. Also on the wall, above the steps which lead down to St Francis' Crypt, is yet another model of an early, possibly Tudor, vessel about which nothing seems to have been recorded. It is a matter of speculation that these could previously have been in other City churches and were transferred here some time between 1948, when the foundation stone for the restoration was laid, and the re-dedication of the church in 1957.

On the north side of the south aisle there are three more models hanging between the triforium arches. That which is nearest the altar is the *Leon*, referred to as a Norwegian Brigantine in some of the guide

The Tudor ship above the steps leading down to the crypt.

books but now thought to be a Swedish timber ship. The offices of the Swedish Chamber of Trade were formerly within the parish of All Hallows, on Tower Hill, and it is probable that they presented the model. She is a two-masted schooner about four feet long and appears to be beautifully carved. As is often the case when models are hung high up it is not possible to examine them in any detail, particularly the deck fittings. The prototype was probably built about 1870–1880.

Next to *Leon* is *Veronica*, a traditional Thames Barge. This is a fully rigged model which commands attention with her long bowsprit and red painted hull with white topsides. She also is about four feet long and was presented by the local firm of Everards, one time barge owners. Her presence here is a good example of the close connections between the church and local companies.

The third triforium arch model is an armed merchantman, of eighteenth century design, though the model is probably Victorian. She is fully rigged, clearly her sails are early and she is possibly of Scandinavian origin. As with other models here, there is no record or provenance. The cannon and some of the fittings (which cannot be seen from the floor) are said to be somewhat over scale, a characteristic of many church ships.

The 'Norwegian' Leon is now thought to be a Swedish timber ship.

There are three more models, all of which have been presented to All Hallows since its restoration. Alongside the stairs, in a glass case, is a fine model of TSMV *Royal Daffodil*. She was a pleasure steamer and one of the fleet of little ships which played such an important part in the evacuation of our troops from Dunkirk in May and June 1940. She was built in 1939 by Denny Brothers and carried over 2000 passengers. The model was the gift of her owners, the General Steam Navigation Co.

On the other side of the passage is the American four-masted clipper ship *Passant of Boston*, a beautiful waterline model with all sails set. She was the gift of Mr H.T. Ainley and his mother 'In Memory of Basil, First Baron Sanderson of Ayot'. Lastly, at present in the undercroft, is the most recent gift, a scale model of HMRC *Vigilant* presented by H.M. Customs and Excise. It is probably unique for a church to have a model of a revenue cutter, but the Custom House is within the parish and, once again, here is a token of the strong links between Church and (a branch of) State. *Vigilant* was built by Brooke Marine of Lowestoft in 1965 and a label in the case gives details of her dimensions and engines.

The All Hallows collection of model ships is unique in British churches and is of great interest to the many visitors. There is clearly scope for some detailed research work to be done on the collection and many of the models would repay expert examination. It may still be possible to discover more about some of them from the church archives.

In the adjacent parish stands the splendidly designated church of St Olave, Hart Street, w. All Hallows Staining and St Catherine Coleman. It is one of the earliest City foundations and is dedicated to St Olav, a Norwegian who helped Ethelred the Unready in the eleventh century. The Norwegian links are still strong and King Haakon laid a foundation stone when the church was re-built after being damaged in the last war. Samuel Pepys the diarist who became Secretary to the Admiralty, is buried here. He was at one time the Master of Trinity House of which St Olave's is the Chaplaincy Church. Since 1514 Trinity House has been responsible for looking after lighthouses and pilotage all around our coasts. It is therefore most appropriate that the Trinity House Chapel should be home to a splendid model of the *Smith Knoll* lightship. Until recently there were over forty manned lightvessels round our coasts, there are now six automatic ones. *Smith Knoll* was one of the last in service, having been replaced by an automatic buoy in the autumn of 1993.

Across the river, in sight of All Hallows, is Southwark Cathedral where there is another model of a Thames barge which was, until recently, on display in the retro-choir. Some years ago the Cathedral had an early model of a Dutch ship of about 1700 which had been presented by the Rt Revd Cuthbert Bardsley when he was Provost. The model was cherished

Veronica is a typical Thames barge, in All Hallows.

An armed merchantman, possibly made early in Victoria's reign hangs next to Veronica.

The Royal Daffodil *took part in the rescue of troops from Dunkirk in 1940. (Photo – Courtesy of Mr Jonathan Green.)*

Passant of Boston *is a fine four-masted American clipper ship. Both the above models are in All Hallows-by-the-Tower.*

and in 1958 it was cleaned, re-painted and re-rigged by the then President of the Society for Nautical Research, Mr Charles Anderson, a noted authority on seventeenth century ships' rigging. The model was later stolen despite being mounted high on the retro-choir wall.

In its place is a model of the Sittingbourne-built sailing barge *Invicta* dating from 1896 and which is on loan to the Cathedral. Until recently this had been temporarily removed for cleaning and restoration but it is now on display in the new (1988) Chapter House Restaurant. Close by there is an interesting historic ship, the *Kathleen and May*, which continued trading until 1960 and is permanently moored in St Mary Overie's dock alongside the Cathedral. She was built in 1900 and is now preserved by the Maritime Trust.

The *Kathleen and May* was until recently berthed in St Katherine's Dock. Until the 1820s, when the dock was built, there had been a Danish mission church on the site. This was demolished and, in 1826, land was donated for its re-building alongside Regent's Park, then being developed by Nash. The present Lutheran Church of St Katherine serves the Danish population in London and is still the place of worship of the visiting seafarers. There are two very splendid model ships in the church, one proudly hanging from the roof towards the west end of the nave, the other stored in the organ loft, The suspended model is a wooden, three-masted, square-rigged trading schooner about four feet long, with what is probably a plank-on-frame built hull. It is one of the few hanging ships which can be looked upon from a gallery, the organ loft, to see the well-made deck details.

Unfortunately she has no name and most of what is known about her derives from oral tradition. She was made in the 1880s by the captain of the ship she represents. On completion he gave the model to his local church in Assen on the isle of Fuenen. After some time, returning from a long voyage, he was dismayed to find that it was still abandoned on the floor. He was upset about this and took it away and presented it to the Danish Seamen's Mission in London. It is known to have been in the Mission at the turn of the century and, when the Mission was closed in 1959, it was transferred to its present home.

St Katherine's has an endearing simplicity and is beautifully lit with elegant chandeliers and a fine east window. The ship model does not dominate but one is always aware of its quiet presence, as a telling reminder of the seafaring heritage of the Danish people.

The other ship is very much larger. Measuring something over seven feet long it is a well detailed model of a four masted square-rigged ship with clipper prow and counter stern. It has a carved female figurehead with a raised right arm and the sails are furled. This ship is also un-named and little is known of its background. It was brought to St

The revenue cutter Vigilant *was presented to All Hallows-by-the-Tower by H.M. Customs and Excise.*

This un-named topsail trading schooner is in the Danish Church of St Katherine in London. She was made by the captain of the ship she represents.

Katherine's after 1959 at the same time as the hanging model and appears not to have been displayed since. There are two long poles fastened alongside the hull and it is possible that these were fitted so that it could be carried in procession. A recent estimate suggests that there are approximately 1500 ship models in Danish churches, the oldest dating from 1610. There it is a custom to hold ship parades, usually when new models are installed or when older ones have been restored. Perhaps such a parade was held at St Katherine's almost thirty five years ago.

Ramsgate, on the eastern tip of the Kent coast has two churches with commemorative models. The Parish Church of Holy Trinity has a fine model of a two masted schooner in a glass case on a window ledge in the south aisle. Measuring some two feet long it is a beautifully detailed model of a (?late Victorian) sailing smack. In 1934, on St Andrew's Day, it was decided to dedicate a part of the north west of the church as a Seamen's Corner. This was a response to the loss with all hands the previous year of the local trawler *Garrigill*. It is thought that the model was among the furnishings offered by local people having a close connection with the sea. There were two further models, an old pulling lifeboat and a steam trawler, both of which are now lost.

Down in the harbour, by the West Pier is the Mission Church which grew out of the Sailors' Home and Harbour Mission. The church was built in 1878 and, through many vissicitudes, has remained open ever since. Since the Seamens' Corner in Holy Trinity was closed in 1979 it has become the centre of worship for the seafaring community and the home of a fine collection of model ships. As often happens where tourism is an important contributor to the local economy such a church becomes an 'attraction' and, in this case the models rather overwhelm the building, making it something of a museum. Many models at the west end of the church are un-named and nothing seems to be known of their provenance. One, the three-masted *Arethusa*, was presented in 1984 by Robert Pope Esq of Rochester, and the commemorative waterline model of the steam trawler *Playmate* has particular significance for the people of Ramsgate. She was commissioned into the Admiralty service in 1939 and was the last ship to leave Calais before the surrender in 1940. Later she was engaged on minesweeping duties in the Thames estuary until the end of the War. It was a great tragedy when she was lost, with all hands, in the great storm of 1953.

There is a small fishermen's chapel in St Ives, Cornwall, which is also a tourist attraction, though services are no longer held there regularly. Neverthless, the chapel of St Leonard is home to an interesting collection of models. The chayple, as it is locally known, is no more than about twelve feet by six feet inside and is situated at the west end of Smeaton's

The beautifully detailed deck fittings of the Danish ship seen from the organ loft.

Pier. It is, however, much older than that and in the sixteenth century was the home of a friar, employed by the fishermen to pray for them. The office seems to have been maintained as late as 1808 when the Rev Warner recorded that the chapel was inhabited by 'a poor fanatic'. The tiny building was restored and re-opened, with a service of blessing, in the summer of 1974 though it is closed during the winter.

During the summer four model boats are displayed there (in winter they are stored in the Guildhall) and all have been made by the well-known local craftsman in wood, Mr Dicon Nance. They are St Ives fishing boats and reflect both the activities of the fishing community and the traditional designs of the boats they used. Each has been made to a scale of 1/24 either to original draughts or from lines taken off original boats. There is the St Ives mackerel boat *Ebenezer*, a Victorian vessel, built in 1868; the model was made to the original drawings. Then there is a local Seine net boat and a St Ives Gig. This was made to lines taken off one of the last gigs by P.J. Oke in 1935. These three models were presented to the Town by the late Mr J. Holman. The fourth model was presented by the maker, Mr Nance, and is a fine model of a St Ives pilchard boat *Godrevy* made to lines he took off the original in 1945.

The collection has the greatest value as an historical record of the activities of the local fishing community and it is in a building which has for centuries been a centre of worship. This contributes to the spiritual atmosphere of what is very much more than a soulless museum.

The model that commemorates the fishing community in Folkestone is not normally kept in the Parish Church of St Peter but is nevertheless closely associated with it. Unusually for this country the model is carried in procession every year during the ceremony of the 'Blessing of the Fisheries'. The Vicar, Father Michael Houghton, has kindly contributed to the following account. On the Sunday after St Peter's Day in July a procession starts from the church on the East Cliff and winds its way down to the Fishing Harbour. Here a service is held, conducted by a visiting Bishop, and the local Salvation Army Band accompanies the hymns. Afterwards the procession re-forms and returns to the cliff top for tea. A focus of attention is a very striking model of a local sailing fishing boat which was made in 1933 and has been carried annually ever since by four boys from the local school wearing traditional fishermen's 'tans'.

At present stored in the organ loft in St Katherine's this large four-masted clipper was possibly used in processions.

During the war the steam drifter Playmate *was used as a minesweeper in the Thames estuary until 1945 and is now celebrated in Ramsgate Harbour's mission church. (Photo – Courtesy of Donald G. Long.)*

The west end of the mission church, Ramsgate, showing the fine collection of decorative model ships. (Photo – Courtesy of Donald G. Long.)

It is a true sailor made model about four feet long overall and was constructed by the second coxwain of the Hastings lifeboat for John Muggridge, the son of one of the local fishermen. It was much treasured and some years ago came into the possession of Mr C. Petts of Folkestone, who is now one of the most senior of the active fishermen. He has looked after the model for many years and has also made some model boats himself.

Named *Good Hope* it carries the local Folkestone registered number FE76 although it is not a scale model of any particular vessel. It is, however, typical of the East Kentish fishing boats, being something of a cross between a Folkestone and a Hastings boat. The model is carried by the four boys with a curiously eerie motion almost as if it were sailing on the water. The cradle is always decorated with flowers by the ladies of the fishing community and is accompanied by a similarly flower-decorated miniature statue of Our Lady of Boulogne seated on the prow of a clinker-built boat. This is a replica of the statue in Boulogne Cathedral, a gift to the parish some years ago, which is emblematic of the shared interests with the maritime communities across the Channel.

In Alderney, perhaps the least visited of the Channel Islands, there is a touching commemorative model in St Anne's church. It is a glass-cased model of the *Fleur de L'Ocean*, a 25 foot Jersey-built crabber, which was involved in an accident off the coast in 1984. The fine model was made soon afterwards by Mr Peter Turreff specifically to remember and commemorate a fourteen-year old boy who was drowned in the accident. In accordance with tradition however, it is also dedicated to 'All the fishermen of Alderney' with the final prayer, 'May God be with them and keep them safe.'

Southampton takes a hard-headed view of its previous role as a great trading port. The Parish Church of St Mary has at present two model ships but is seeking to have them transferred to the Southampton Maritime Museum when the new premises are completed. They are modern shipbuilders' models in glass cases and it is true that they do not have quite the same appeal as the earlier thankofferings. The models are of the RMMV *Winchester Castle*, built in 1931, and HMS *Jersey*. They were both presented when the church was re-built in 1954, in time for the dedication of the Seamen's Chapel in 1956. Both models are in good condition, but the Vicar says that they are no longer felt to have the same significance that they once did now that the maritime connections have been so weakened. The church still has its binnacle lectern in the Seamens' Chapel, similar to that at St Leonards-on-Sea.

From the middle of the nineteenth century until the 1930s the port of Brixham on the south coast was the centre of an extensive fishing industry.

The sailing smacks were known all around our coasts. In 1850 there were 210 Brixham trawlers and they fished the Bristol Channel, the Irish Sea, Dublin Bay and the North Sea. Today only one, the *Provident* remains, preserved and the pride of the Island Cruising Club's fleet. The club's headquarters are in Salcombe, Devon where, in the parish church of Holy Trinity a model of a typical Brixham smack hangs from the nave roof. It was made in the mid-1930s by an unknown seaman who sailed on a similar vessel, a sister ship to the *Provident*. The model was given to the Island Cruising Club when the maker died a few years ago. Since the Club had no suitable place to display it the vicar, the Revd Abram, thought that the church would be an appropriate place. For some time it had been in the care of the well-known local model shipwright Malcolm Darch. Although the model is far below Malcolm's usual standards of workmanship he repaired and restored it with great sensitivity so that it retains the spirit of the original.

The trawler is numbered BM17 and is named, on the stern, *Heather Ann, Brixham*. No records exist either of this number or of the name so it seems possible that the maker named her after his own fancy. She measures about three feet overall and is very well rigged with navigation lights, galley stove pipe, nets, buckets and nicely detailed traditional sails. She is one of the few hanging church ships that can be looked down upon from a gallery and she is also a living ship since it was due to Malcolm Darch that she hangs from a single wire so that there are subtle movements in the gentle draughts when doors are opened.

The Cornish village of Veryan can be approached by a devious road from Truro or, more interestingly, by the King Harry Ferry from Falmouth. It is well known for its round houses which guard the approaches to the village, reputedly to confuse the Devil, should he come prowling round. The Parish Church is dedicated to an obscure saint from which the village itself derives its name. St Symphorian was a 3rd century martyr beheaded at Autun in France for refusing to honour pagan gods. Why he should be venerated in a Cornish village is not clear but the Church is home to a notable model ship. This is an elegant three-masted trading schooner with clipper prow and counter stern. The prototype was the *Olivebank*, built in 1892 and perhaps the most famous of all the Bank Line sailing ships. She was still afloat, under the Finnish flag, until the second world war.

It is a beautiful model, about two feet long, with what appears to be a carved bone figurehead and is carefully preserved in a glass case on the south wall near the door. The *Olivebank* was presented to the church in 1936 by the then vicar, the Revd E.C. Alston. There is no record of the maker but it is possible that it was Mr Alston himself. Unusually, the model does not commemorate the vessel itself – she was still working in

The Olivebank *was the most elegant of the Bank Line sailing ships. She is in the Church of St Symphorian, Veryan near Falmouth, and commemorates those who lost their lives in shipwrecks round adjacent coasts.*

the mid-1930s – but is preserved as a representative ship to honour the memories of all the men who lost their lives round the local coasts. It is the custom for a large bowl of flowers to stand on the top of the case.

The Parish Church of Zennor is on the site of a sixth century Celtic church and is dedicated to St Senara, another legendary saint about whom little is known historically. The present church, much restored in 1890, has a barrel vaulted nave, built in the tradition of an upturned ship. It is perhaps best known for the medieval carved mermaid chair. She holds a looking glass in her right hand and a comb in her left, a classical symbol in the Middle Ages of the human and divine natures of Christ. In a corner of the nave, alongside the organ, hangs a most atmospheric model of a two-masted Cornish trading schooner. It has the appearance of an early-to mid-Victorian model with a delightfully patinated green copper coloured hull. As is so often the case with these models no maker is recorded but it would seem that it is considerably older than the date of its presentation. It was given in loving memory of Mr W.A. Proctor who was born in 1913 and who was lost in the Pacific Ocean on a single-

A characteristic Cornish trading schooner hangs serenely in St Senara's Church in Zennor, Cornwall. She, too, commemorates local mariners and was placed 'In remembrance of the sailors shipwrecked on the coast who lie un-named in the churchyard'.

handed voyage from Newlyn in 1965. It also serves as 'a token of rememberance to the sailors shipwrecked on this coast who lie un-named in the churchyard'.

It is a typical, and quite delightful, hanging church ship. To find it here, on the western tip of Cornwall in a village beginning with Z, was a great pleasure and it seems appropriate that it should be the last one to be described.

7

Conclusion

During the course of this study it has not been possible to visit more than a fraction of the 10,000-plus churches and chapels in this country. Hopefully, in the future, many more ship models will be brought to light. Some will already be proudly displayed but will have been overlooked whilst others will be found abandoned in dark corners from which they may be rescued and put in places of honour. If the reasons for their presence can be discovered and recorded this will add to their historical value.

Despite the limitations of a pioneer study some tentative conclusions can be reached based on those ship models examined so far. Some are obvious, others less so. First of all, as might be expected, the majority of church ships are in coastal towns and villages, or in those places having a particularly close relationship with the sea. Secondly, they are to be found in very diverse locations, from Canterbury Cathedral and York Minster to a humble and almost deserted chapel in St Ives in Cornwall. It has come as some surprise that few have been found in Wales and that churches on the Isle of Man or on the Orkney or Shetland Islands do not appear to possess any. This latter is curious in view of the Scandinavian influence there and the large numbers which are cherished in Danish, Norwegian and Swedish churches.

There seems to be little connection between the dedications of churches and the presence of ship models. Many of the coastal churches are dedicated to locally revered saints who did not necessarily have anything to do with the sea. St Hilda (South Shields) who was born in Northumbria and St Edmund (Southwold) who was king of the Angles are two examples. It might be thought that many ships would be associated with the apostles St Peter, St Andrew and St John who were among the Galilean fishermen but this does not appear to be so. St Nicholas is considered the patron saint of mariners and merchants and is credited in popular tradition with saving some sailors who were in distress off the Lycian coast. However, of the churches and chapels dedicated to him only the Devonport naval chapel, Christ Church, North Shields, Liverpool Parish (Our Lady and St Nicholas) and the Hastings fishermen's chapel have models.

F. and C. Boullet, in their authoritative book *'Ex-Voto Marins'* published in Paris in 1978, have indicated that in Western European countries there is little difference in numbers between those to be found in predominantly Protestant and those in Roman Catholic churches. Here, however, general enquiries so far have revealed none in Roman Catholic churches or cathedrals. The Church of England has the majority whilst the rest are in Non-Conformist churches and chapels. This is in line with a recent survey done in Holland by Dr J.M.G. van der Poel in his book *Scheepsmodellen in Nederlandse Kirken* published by the Institute for Church Art in the Netherlands.

The ships that have inspired model makers were built at almost any time in the past and some recent models are of quite ancient vessels. There are more examples of contemporary church ships, ie, those made at the time of their prototypes, than might be expected. We have seen that those from the seventeenth century are mostly in museums but there are many eighteenth and nineteenth century models still in their churches. It is particularly interesting that many have been made in this century, notably in the 1920s and the 1950s, and that they are still being made. The models themselves have been very diverse both in the types of vessels taken and in the craftsmanship displayed in their construction. The typical sailor made model, lovingly carved and finished on a long voyage, was not often true to scale but was invariably true to the spirit of the ship. Since many are hung high in the roofs of churches it is often difficult to see them closely. One, however, the Brixham trawler in Salcombe Parish Church, Devon, (See page 70) can be looked down upon from a gallery where it is possible to see a rich collection of rigging, ropes, buckets and navigation lights as well as fishing nets and a galley stove pipe.

The larger models, often made by professional craftsmen or highly skilled and devoted amateurs, have hulls built upon frames with proper miniature planking just as their prototypes. Smaller ones are often carved from either solid blocks of wood or from three or four thick planks, roughly shaped and then glued together. These are called 'bread and butter' hulls. It is probable that many of the solid wooden ones, known as 'blocks' in the eighteenth century, were made during long and tedious voyages which often lasted for years. Although tools were often limited excellent ship models could be made with knives and a few files.

The majority of prototypes are sailing vessels, even for those models built recently. This is surely because such ships are more beautiful to our eyes than later power driven ones. For instance, the model of HMS *Canterbury* in Canterbury Cathedral is modelled on the first ship, built in the eighteenth century, although it was made in the 1930s and commemorates the last vessel of that name which was taken out of commission in 1933.

Modelling ships was only one of a number of shipboard crafts practised during off-duty times using fairly crude raw materials which were readily to hand. Among sailors' specialities were elaborate woollen embroidered pictures, and scrimshaw work, the primitive scratched pictures on whalebone and walrus ivory which are now much collected and, sadly, faked. Ornamental and useful object such as mats were made from rope, elaborately woven and knotted. There was also the highly developed craft of making and inserting ship models in bottles. This is a practice which started in the early nineteenth century and which carries certain lore of its own. The sailor was in effect capturing the spirit of his ship and preserving it; he was corking up the memory of fair breezes and blue seas for his own comfort and, in turn, left them behind with his family and friends as a talisman against his safe return. Such bottled ships do not appear in churches, probably only because, by their very nature, they were too small to be properly appreciated in naves or chancels.

However knowledgeable seamen are about winds and tides their ships are always at risk from storms and tempests. Sailing ships in the past were particularly vulnerable and many of the church models represent vessels which did not survive the perils of the deep. The congregations, now and in the past, have always included families and friends intimately associated with the fates of those on board the vessels whose models are enshrined in their places of worship. Their prayers and meditations are helped by the presence of evocative miniatures. About a third of the models described in this book are hung from the roof beams. In this they follow the usual practice in the Netherlands where those fastened to walls or in glass cases are considered inferior. There is an indefinable magic about ships suspended, as it were, between heaven and earth and which are seen from a fish-eye viewpoint. They have a tranquillity and a serenity which is only heightened by their imperceptible movements. Their crews may have a turbulent life at sea but in church all are reminded that there is also peace and calm.

It is only when this is borne in mind that their significance can be properly understood. All church models, in their several ways, have been offered to the glory of God through the hands and skills of the craftsmen who made them. Among the many examples in this book we have recorded two from modern times which stand out with particulary poignancy. Both were sailor made, both were given in thanks to God, the one by a seaman steeped in a remote island tradition, the other lovingly made by a devout and skilled modelmaker.

The first is the touching model of one of the frail fishing boats still used round the island of Tristan da Cunha. This was made by one of the temporary refugees from the volcano which made the islanders' homes uninhabitable in the 1960s. Those who were accommodated near Bletchingley in Sussex wanted to express their gratitude to the local people for the kind and welcoming way in which they had been received. Using the simple materials which were available at home, one of the pensioners made a model from memory and it was presented to St Mary's at a farewell party for the community before they returned to Tristan da Cunha. Carefully preserved in a glass case the engraved plaque reads

To the Parish of St Mary the Virgin, Bletchingley,
from the people of Tristan da Cunha in Gratitude.
1961 – 1962

The other special modern votive model was that made and presented by Commander Peter Clissold to his parish church. He was a man of deep piety who loved the sea and all its traditions and in later life made a study of naval memorials in churches and chapels around the Solent. He took some years over the creation of his model of HMS *Hotspur* which he offered to the church of St Mary, Hook-with-Warsash, in Hampshire. The simple and unaffected dedication speaks for all ship models, in every cathedral, church and chapel which have been given, as was Peter Clissold's –

TO THE GLORY OF GOD
And in thankfulness for blessings received
on sea and on shore.

Index to Locations

Italic figures refer to illustrations